Skin Game

Caroline Kettlewell

St. Martin's Griffin
New York

Book design by Ellen R. Sasahara

Library of Congress Cataloging-in-Publication Data

Kettlewell, Caroline.
    Skin game / Caroline Kettlewell
        p.   cm.
    ISBN 0-312-20011-0 (hc)
    ISBN 0-312-26393-7 (pbk)
    1. Kettlewell, Caroline.   2. Self-mutilation—Patients—Virginia
Biography.   I. Title.
RC552.S4K48   1999
616.85'82—dc21
    [B]   99-20945
                                                                           CIP

10 9

To my mother, with love and appreciation

Tomorrow is a new day. You shall begin it well and serenely and with too high a spirit to be encumbered with your old nonsense.

RALPH WALDO EMERSON

Part One

Skin has a good memory. Skin is like the ground we
walk every day; you can read a whole history in it
if you know how to look.

1

One February day in the seventh grade, I was apprehended in the girls' bathroom at school, trying to cut my arm with my Swiss Army knife. It is always February in the seventh grade, that terrible border year, that dangerous liminal interlude.

I was apprehended in the girls' bathroom, in the act—to be precise—of wearing at my arm with the saw blade of my Swiss Army knife.

Until the moment of my apprehension, I didn't once think, *People will find this odd.* How could they? Is there nothing more fascinating than our own blood? The scarlet beauty of it. The pulsing immediacy. The way it courses through its endless circuit of comings and goings, slipping and rushing and seeping down to the cells of us, the intimate insider that knows all the news, that's been down to the mailroom and up to the boardroom.

In Mr. Davidson's biology class, the air dry with winter heat and pricked by the smell of formaldehyde and decay, we had been peering at mounted samples of unknown origin pressed flat between glass slides—papery shreds of tissue and muddy blotches of long-dried blood. And I got the idea that it would be more interesting to examine my own blood under the microscope. Blood still wet, still rich with urgent color. I imagined lively, plump little corpuscles tumbling against each other like a miniature game of bumper cars.

Everything is perfectly clear when looked at in the right light; I chose the school bathroom for my theater of operations because if you want your blood to be fresh to the task, you have to be handy to the microscope when you bring it forth. I had brought my Swiss Army knife to school precisely for this purpose. It was recess. I would cut, and then I would quickstep down the hall to Mr. Davidson's classroom—with its shelves crowded with chunks of rock and skeletal remains and things floating pickled in Ball jars—and screw down the probing eye of 10× magnification onto the very essence of my own self.

I found this plan so compelling it blinded me to other thought. The idea of the blood beckoned to me, hypnotic and seductive. How often do we know the blood of our veins? It reveals itself to us only as the herald of bad news: the injury, the illness, the sudden slip of the paring knife or the prick of the doctor's needle. Why should we meet only in disaster?

It wasn't as big a leap as you might imagine. I'd never been blood squeamish. I proudly displayed my scabs and scars, vaguely envious of my older sister, who seemed to garner all the really good injuries, the satisfyingly dramatic ones that needed stitches, and constructions of gauze and splint and tape, and shots and salves to ward off deliciously hideous consequences: lockjaw, sepsis, gangrene.

———

The key to success is to envision the thing in your mind. Draw the bright chrome of the blade along the slender rope of vein wrapping sinuous around your left wrist, and everything parts obediently beneath your command, like the Red Sea before Moses.

Except it didn't. The knife blade was worn too dull, as dull as the dun walls of the bathroom where I stood. With my arm braced against the warm metal shelf over a radiator, I could see the veins meandering blue and purple and green like a road map beneath the thin cover of my flesh. Only the frailest membrane of tissue keeping self from self. Yet who would have thought that skin could have so much substance, so much resistance?

I attempted and discarded in quick succession the can opener, the leather punch, and the flathead screwdriver. I settled at length on the saw blade, an unhappy compromise. It scraped back and forth like a fiddler's bow against my arm, chafing the skin red and raw. Little white clumps of flesh gummed up the blade, and the stubborn shelter of my skin refused to give way.

The radiator clanked and hissed. The bathroom smelled of disinfectant and body functions. I stood there and sawed. I wasn't doing a very good job of it, because sawing on your arm hurts. It burns. Disappointingly clumsy and painful and blundering, it was nothing like the swift, precise operation I had imagined.

To compound matters, I gathered a tiresome audience of other girls. You know, the popular girls. The typecast antagonists of the after-school movie. The ones who have always found that life just happens to be in perfect agreement with their opinions.

"Eeeuhhh. What are you doing?"

"I'm trying to cut myself," I said.

"Why?"

"Because I want to."

"That's really disgusting," said one.

"She just wants attention," muttered another darkly.

But still they stood about, like rubberneckers at a train wreck. After so many years of recesses, after all, what excitements are left? You have fifteen minutes, and you have to kill them somehow.

"You're going to get in trouble for this," announced the ringleader at last, rendering her verdict with a self-satisfied toss of her confident head, before guaranteeing the outcome by retreating to alert the authorities.

In the intricately nuanced grade-school hierarchy I wasn't one of those popular girls, the ones born to straight teeth and straight hair and genetically predetermined self-confidence. I wasn't one of the outcasts either—the pale kids with the weird health problems, or the ones who always said the wrong thing at the wrong time and didn't even know it, or the ones whose mothers made them liverwurst sandwiches for lunch. I had always occupied the shifting territory of the middle ground, sunk low by my hopeless ineptitude at all sports involving a ball, raised up by my standing as one of the smart kids.

I'd slid by on smart. I'd made smart do in the place of industry and application. As far back as nursery school my teacher had noted on my report card that *Caroline loves to volunteer information,* but *Her attention span is quite easily distracted* and *She has no incentive to accomplish a finished or well-done paper.* I never took naturally to the linearity of school, the ordered progression of hours and ideas. My mind has always raced about with the distracted enthusiasm of a dog chasing squirrels, pursuing one idea, then whirling after another, and sometimes losing itself staring up along the endlessly branching pathways down which the last idea has fled. I stared out windows, daydreaming. I doodled. I read books tucked surreptitiously within the covers of whatever textbook we were meant to be following. I got by on last-minute efforts—and what's worse, I knew I could.

I got my comeuppance in sixth grade, when I was demoted to the slow-learning section for having what my school termed "a poor attitude." They didn't call it the slow-learning section, of course—B^1 is what they called it, as distinguished from A, or, more direly, B^2—but we were none of us so slow-witted that we couldn't figure it out.

I remember feeling at the time of my demotion that some inevitable truth had at last come out. I come from a family of scholars and educators, and I think I've long suffered a sneaking suspicion that I've never quite measured up to the high standard of intellectual rigor valued above all else by my relations.

I can't remember a time, in fact, when I didn't think I was coming up short in one regard or another. Through no fault of her own my sister, two years older, had served as the measure by which my inadequacies were perpetually thrown into relief. She was better at sports, better at board games, better at drawing and painting and projects, more musical, more popular, and, of course, smarter.

"Oh, you're *Julia's* little sister," her former teachers would say to me, the first day I entered their classes at the beginning of a school year, and though I felt a swelling of pride by association, I could see already how there was no hope of proving adequate to all the expectations implied by that statement. In the first grade, according to the report by the administrator of an IQ test I took then, I kept repeating, "Oh, stupid me, that's wrong," and "I'm stupid and I can't do this."

The demotion to B^1 had the quality, therefore, of a long-expected if dreaded inevitability. I even remember reassuring my parents, when the school informed us of my new class placement, that it was probably the best thing anyway.

For the better part of the day they sequestered us, the hopeless and the hapless of the B^1, in a subterranean cinder-block dungeon of a classroom, its walls painted a psychosis-inducing shade of dingy yellow, its only window a narrow slit high in the wall, through which we could see the occasional passage of a knee-socked leg on the playground above. Our teacher had tried to invest the room with some faint cheer by taping up those droll little posters of bedraggled kittens and antic orangutans, captioned "Don't bother me, I'm having a bad day" or "No more monkeying around."

We were all, always, having a bad day in B^1, or so it seemed. We snarled and sniped at each other, flinging invective, muttering mutinously. Every few weeks or so we were treated to a visit from the headmaster or the middle-school director, whose sole purpose in coming was to lecture us on our utter failure to live up to even the most nominal and rudimentary standards of decency and respectability, and the imminent likelihood that our entire school's reputation would be laid low by our sorry collective performance.

I have no memory at all of what we did to earn ourselves such administrative enmity, but I felt marooned in a savage land. Though mine was a small school, I swear I never saw or spoke again to any of my former comrades in A, and at the same time I felt as though my B[1] classmates regarded me contemptuously as a fallen member of a corrupt aristocracy. I'd been exiled by the unforgiving academic caste system: a student without a country.

2

I'd managed to wear no more than a raw, angry, two-inch abrasion into my arm when, as forecast, I got in trouble. Mrs. Warren, the middle-school director, marched briskly into the bathroom, her heels tapping smartly on the gray ceramic tile.

"What are you doing!" she demanded in a low, ominous voice. Less a question than an indication of trouble to come.

What was I going to say? What I was actually doing was self-evident. She was asking, really, not what was I doing, but instead what was the meaning of what I was doing. And whatever the answer to that question might be, it was already obvious to me, in that instant, that no answer was going to constitute sufficient justification for my actions.

I flushed with guilt, as if I'd been caught in the act of some smutty gutter sin, feeling that panicky regret of childhood, when what you thought was a fantastic, a delightful idea goes suddenly wrong, and it occurs to you for the first time, like a revelation, that it was an idea the grownups would have been against from the get-go.

Because you know that when teachers ask, "What are you doing?," they don't really want an answer. They want you to skip right over the explication of the plot and get directly to the heartfelt confession of your sins. They only ask you what you're doing, after all, when you're doing something they think you ought not be doing.

So of course I ended up in the Office, the court of high crimes and misdemeanors alike. Be it discipline or disaster, when in doubt, marshal the forces in the Office.

I was hustled down the hall, past clumps of middle-schoolers doing a bad job of pretending not to be watching, and into Mrs. Warren's office, where the principal and the school nurse and my homeroom teacher sat in attendance. They ranged themselves in a semicircle of leather seats worn with age, which creaked and crackled with every movement. I perched uncomfortably in an armchair before them, my arms and legs twisted into pretzels of self-consciousness. If they had meant to suggest solicitous concern, to invite my halting confidences, they missed their mark. All the scene would have required was a fierce light blinding my eyes to resemble the interrogation sequence in a thriller.

The grilling commenced, a long afternoon of judicial inquiry in which I was meant to serve at once as both the star witness and the chief suspect, whose job it was to help identify the crime, illuminate the motive, and elicit the confession, all before the bell rang to signal the end of the school day. My confiscated knife—Exhibit A—passed from hand to hand. Heads were shaken in dismay. Questions probed me like insinuating fingers.

"Would you like to tell us about this?" they asked.

———

I found myself in a delicate position. I've always been a sucker for an audience, any audience. While the present situation was uncomfortable and even nerve-racking with its disciplinary overtones, still there was no denying I had myself an audience, four adults gazing at me with rapt anticipation. And I could feel the almost irresistible temptation to offer them something worth their while. Not to fabricate, precisely, but to nip and tuck at the details until I had made for them something more compelling than the truth.

The plain fact of it was that I was miserable—though my misery wasn't so much sadness as it was a shrieking unease, a gnawing despair, which I had been trying that morning to cut out of myself.

I knew how I felt, but I couldn't come up with a good enough reason why I should feel that way. I believed unhappiness was something you had to earn through a suitable measure of suffering, the way the characters in my favorite books struggled with blindness, polio, Nazis, shipwreck, blizzards—unspeakable adversities through which, damaged but undefeated, they endured. And what had I ever suffered? Not one damn thing. No poetic privations or romantic diseases. The way I saw it, my life—with its twelve-year-old particulars of tuna sandwiches and math homework and watching *The Waltons* on Thursday nights—was way too mundane for suffering.

I'll admit that suffering, or rather, the dramatic interest of being One Who Suffered, appealed to me. I could see myself tragic and tortured, wasted by some suitably novel madness or malaise that would leave me wanly luminous, a brave inspiration to friends and family gathered about my bedside. (Against all professional predictions I'd make a spirited and miraculous recovery in time for the final commercial break.)

Life had cast me, however, for another role. I was the contract player, the antic sidekick, the supporting chorus, and it was only the lead players whose troubles counted in the plot. I'd be the quirky best friend in a movie, but never the love interest; I'd be Sally in *The Dick Van Dyke Show,* but never Laura Petrie. When parts were handed out, my sister was called as the ingenue—emotionally delicate, quixotic, and temperamental—while I'd been cued as a Falstaff, forever bumbling about on the sidelines.

Whether we'd chosen those roles, or whether we'd fallen into them by chance, or whether I was the only one who ever even saw them that way, to me these positions seemed as inevitable and inalterable as time itself. My sister might falter under the burden of troubles I couldn't hope to understand, but unhappiness would never be written into my character sketch.

What I was feeling, anyway—it wasn't nearly interesting enough to be true and tragic unhappiness. It felt neither romantic nor dramatic nor poetic, but rather grinding and unpleasant, like a sore throat. I was highly suspicious of it, thinking it might, after all, be nothing more than a self-indulgent pettishness, just another way I was trying to copy my sister, like the way I'd taken up the flute after she did.

My situation appeared to me like the continuous, twisting loop of a Möbius strip: I wanted to be tragic in order to justify simply being unhappy, but knowing that I wanted to be tragic made me suspect the very legitimacy of that unhappiness. My unhappiness was a guilty secret, and I thought if I confessed to it I would be roundly denounced, as though I'd cribbed from someone else's test or stolen from my sister's closet.

"What right have you to pretend to unhappiness?" they would demand, and I would have no answer.

If someone in authority, however, someone who had the power to grant such things, might allow my unhappiness, then it would at last bear the stamp of legitimacy, and I would be free to believe in it. Only—and here the Möbius strip carried me back again to the beginning—I couldn't imagine convincing the Authorities of my unhappiness without having some real and substantive cause to point to, and I had no such cause, so wouldn't that mean that if they believed me, then I had succeeded only in perpetrating a fraud?

I had been mulling over this conundrum for months, ever since this wretchedness had insinuated itself into my life like a poisonous mold, putting out little creeping tentacles until all of me was taken over with it. Now, confronted finally with an opportunity to tell all, I knew I wouldn't have the courage to try. I couldn't bear to face their disappointment in me for being so ridiculous and fanciful and self-indulgent as to imagine I could ever be truly unhappy.

———————

"Why were you cutting yourself?" Mrs. Warren asked, and all I could say was "I don't know."

I *did* know, but what I knew I couldn't explain. I was trying to cut myself. I wanted to cut for the cut itself, for the delicate severing of capillaries, the transgression of veins. I needed to cut the way your lungs scream for air when you swim the length of the pool underwater in one breath. It was a craving so organic it seemed to have arisen from my skin itself. Imagining the sticky-slick scarlet trails of my own blood soothed me.

This made no sense, and yet it was the truth. How was I, at twelve, going to explain it?

I tried to tell them about biology class, about wanting to examine my own blood cells. That didn't sound unreasonable. That sounded like the kind of wacky thing a kid might do in the name of scientific inquiry, like eating bugs or melting crayons in the toaster oven. I tried to tell them but they wouldn't buy it, this answer closest to the truth. It wasn't the answer they wanted.

"I'm really sorry," I ended up saying, over and over, hoping my apology would make the whole thing go away. "I won't do it again." Now I just wanted the afternoon to be done with, my knife returned, everyone back to their familiar relationships and routines.

Only they wouldn't let it go.

"Why?" they kept asking. "Why?"

They tossed theories at me like softballs, hoping I'd swing at one. Blood pacts. TV movies. Ideas that girls got in their heads, sometimes, when they read too many teenage novels.

"Maybe you just wanted some attention," they suggested—the conclusion, I suspect, they'd already formulated. They hailed from the seen-and-not-heard school of child-rearing; their job as educators was to stamp the savage out of us and subdue us into quiescence, and some of us, like me, were not coming along too promisingly. I was an attention-grabber and hogger of spotlights, no denying. One of those kids who's always waving her hand frantically, straining from her seat in the hope of being called upon, one who's not above casually embellishing the dull facts of a story to liven it up for the audience.

When I'd planned out the idea of cutting myself, however, it had never once occurred to me that I would excite the least notice, though now I could see, of course, that this selective blindness had been precisely the fatal flaw in my plan.

"Maybe you should see someone," they sighed at last.

"Maybe," I mumbled.

Someone, someday, somehow—it was a good answer all around, full of possibility, devoid of substance. It made me look cooperative. It made them look helpful. It relieved all of us of any obligation actually to do anything further, and then they could just send me home early, the resolution something of a toss-up between a sick day and a suspension. They even, as I had hoped, gave me my knife back.

My mother was called to fetch me. To have your mother called meant you were either sick or in trouble, and I wasn't sick. I waited in dread for her arrival, but she was whisked right past me into the office.

Behind closed doors, the matter was discussed with her. I was not invited to participate. Instead, I waited awkwardly in the hall outside Mrs. Warren's office as my classmates filed past between classes, some stopping to whisper eagerly, "Did you get in all kinds of trouble?"

I have no idea what was said in that conference. I've never asked my mother. Did they lay blame? Downplay and dismiss? Did they suggest to my mother that here was another case of Caroline trying to hog the center stage? That's the possibility I'd lay my wager on.

———

At last my mother emerged, and in uncomfortable silence we walked the length of the hallway and then crunched across the gravel parking lot to our car. Low clouds scudded overhead, and a damp wind whipped at our clothes.

"What were you doing?" she asked at last.

"I don't know," I said.

"You won't do it again?" she asked.

"No," I said.

Which one of us did I lie to protect?

We become who we are through an intricate warp and weft of inheritance and experience too tightly interwoven ever to come unbound. If you could follow any one thread, unweave the patterns, where would it lead you?

I will tell you three stories of my family:

My mother grew up in a Boston suburb of neat homes and clipped lawns, playing field hockey, walking to school, eating ice cream at Brigham's. She spent summers in cheerless camps in the company of Mayflower descendants, where Spartan conditions and an exhausting, almost continual round of sports were meant to instill the backbone of nation-builders. Sundays, her family bathed in the rarefied, minimalist creeds of the Unitarian church. Her father had a profession in the city. Her mother stood watch over a kitchen where no crumb dared stray.

My mother always felt as though her family's life, in every particular, was like a backlot movie set assembled to paint an illusion, and she kept wondering when the audience would step through a door or around a corner and discover the jury-rigged assemblage of scaffolding propping the whole thing up. My grandparents were first-generation Americans, and as with so many of their kind and their generation, the entire structure of their adult lives was meant as denial of that fact.

"Masters of ethnic cleansing," a friend of my mother calls them.

My grandmother had grown up in a grindingly poor working-class Irish family, under the shadow of a drunken father, amid domestic chaos and constant reminders of the impending threat of a Catholic hell. My grandfather was an English Jew. Educated, professional, nonpracticing, but inescapably a Jew. My grandparents' families never forgave them for marrying each other, but with one stroke the two of them severed themselves from the strangling umbilici of their childhoods, and set out to remake themselves as Americans by Norman Rockwell. In my mother's childhood, my grandmother's earlier poverty and my grandfather's Jewishness were the dark, unmentionable secrets to be suffocated beneath the weight of tree-lined suburban streets and exquisitely modern appliances.

My mother felt formless and groundless in this household, where her family's only identity was a rigorous nonidentity, where they marked themselves only by who they weren't, leaving unanswered the question of who they were.

———————

My father's father was a wielder of words, and in the Second World War he served as spin doctor to the Navy; at my father's house now I can thumb through a stack of glossy eight-by-ten black-and-white official-issue photographs, my grandfather standing on some carrier deck or airport tarmac, beaming in the company of Nimitz, of Eisenhower.

My father's father was not, by nature, a man to be persuaded by anyone's opinion but his own. He referred to himself always in the third person, the central character in what amounted to the one-man show of his life; all the rest of his family labored anonymously in the chorus, meant to hum harmony to his solos.

In my father's childhood, my grandfather took up and abandoned with equal precipitousness one lucrative job after another. For a time the family would live in luxurious, twelve-room Chicago waterfront apartments with maids and doormen and a smartly dressed attendant to bring the car around when they went out for a drive. Then my grandfather would quit in high dudgeon over some perceived slight or an uncompromisable difference of opinion, and the family's fortunes would dwindle until they were reduced to cramped walk-up flats and thrice-darned socks, when finally my grandfather, full of grand plans and empty promises, would allow himself to be lured into some new vice presidency or directorship of sales. My father and his twin brother changed schools eight times before the sixth grade.

Their standing in the world was so entirely peripatetic that it was hard to know at any given time if they were keeping up appearances or living below their means, whether they were being imprudently extravagant or needlessly thrifty. On some days my father and uncle might come home to find their father wardrobing them from the Salvation Army; on others, to discover that he had magnanimously distributed all their toys to poor children.

After my parents married, they moved to Illinois, where my father had been hired to serve as rector of an Episcopal church in a Chicago bedroom community that whispered its wealth discreetly in the details of ordinary life—authentic Oriental rugs, private schools, perfectly manicured lawns.

Early each morning the women deposited their men at the train station for the commute to Chicago; money was made in grain futures, corporate law, investment banking. The women's lives were occupied with overseeing the army of service people who maintained their immaculate homes and gardens, with raising the next generation of polite, socially poised, well-scrubbed children, and with attending to a variety of good works. It was a world of exquisite understatement, of flawless entertaining, with perfectly mannered children making brief, freshly bathed appearances at dinner parties before being tucked into bed, of faultlessly orchestrated charity events.

To the members of the church board who had hired my father, my parents must have seemed very much the right sort. My father was a Harvard man. My mother hailed from that unassailable Boston suburb, knew which fork to use with the fish course.

But my parents were neither manicured nor restrained, a fact they felt obliged to keep within the rambling confines of the rectory where we lived. They were feet-up-on-the-furniture people, raucous intellectuals, Kennedy Democrats. My mother had fled that Boston suburb as a dissident escapes a repressive regime. My father had made his way through Harvard washing his laundry in the sink, working summers in a candy factory. Our home was threadbare, with thrift-store-salvaged Oriental carpeting, and chairs that welcomed slouching, and my sister and me racketing around the house shrieking and strewing toys. Like my father's parishioners, our family repaired to a vacation home on Lake Michigan, but ours was a ramshackle cabin, with temperamental homemade plumbing, which my father and his twin brother had paid for with summer jobs and slapped up in the mosquito-infested woods the year they turned fifteen.

My father had no particular gift for cocktail party chatter, the oil that lubricated the machinery of his parish life. He couldn't keep people's names straight, did not much care about the vicissitudes and vagaries of Business in the City. He'd suddenly recall that the vestry meeting had started fifteen minutes ago, that he'd said yes to a luncheon for this afternoon. He was wholly guileless in these lapses, his mind already again somewhere else, too restless to alight on any one matter for longer than a moment.

My mother, disappointed in a church that relegated women to bustling around the periphery with covered dishes and silver polish, had left Yale Divinity School, where she was studying theology, to marry my father. ("You'll be poor all your life!" cried my grandmother in protest when my mother broke the news of her engagement.) But in Illinois, with abstruse theological discourse still echoing in her ears, my mother found herself expected to make her way as the rector's wife, in attendance upon women whose entire lives—their homes, their children, their accomplishments—were meant to serve as tributes to their husbands' success.

My mother found these women gracious, generous, and thoroughly intimidating. My father conscientiously attended to his duties as parish priest, but felt quixotically more at home among the lifers he tutored each week at the state penitentiary, following the true calling of his Christianity to minister to the least among us.

My parents' tenure in Illinois was marked by the uncomfortable feeling, says my mother, that they were masquerading in the guise of their apparent qualifications—that Harvard degree, those Boston bona fides—and expecting at every moment to be unmasked.

What I'm trying to say is that my family has a history of living lives of fabrication, and after a while it comes to seem natural to edit freely. And if you could pick and choose, wouldn't it be tempting simply to elide what is least pleasant? In my family, we had so profoundly lost the language for anger or unhappiness or despair, for the awkward and the uncomfortable and the unpleasant, that we didn't even know something was missing. In the home where I grew up, no one ever argued. No one ever yelled, except every now and then my sister—and then we all would look politely away as if it were something she couldn't help, like Tourette's, like epilepsy.

It's not that we lived in a strained silence of the unspoken. To the contrary, we went for words in a big way—scads of words, volumes of words; we would never have been content to buy just one vowel from Pat Sajak. We lived amid piles of books and cascading heaps of *New Yorkers* next to every chair and bed.

With our language creating a diversion, however, we looked the other way, like people whistling past a graveyard. There was something out there, something you couldn't dare to acknowledge:

a writhing Pandora's box of frustrations determinedly quashed, angry words bitten back, sorrows unvoiced. It could bring down the world if opened. Instead, our words kept the lid on, smoothing cleanly, invisibly over the gaps, an unconscious habit of indirection. No one would ever be so presumptuous as to ask about your troubles, and you would never be so presumptuous as to tell.

On the drive home from school on that February day in 1975, my mother and I would have spoken of other matters. I wouldn't have known how to tell the plain and simple truth. The truth seemed the most dangerous, the most damning admission, the one I couldn't allow for.

4

The funny thing about silence is that it always makes the thing not mentioned seem as though it must be so much worse than you imagined.

The day after my school bathroom debacle I went back to school, because what else are you going to do? You go on in life because another day rolls around and expects things of you.

My seventh-grade sociopathic classmates had a field day with the whole affair, smacking as it did of the unforgivable sin of self-importance. I'd called attention to myself—did I think I was something special? Did I think I was better than anyone else? The logic of these accusations was hazy, but the impact powerful. My tormentors deployed them like stealth weapons, the stiletto in the back of the neck to the unsuspecting victim.

"Oh, go slit your wrists," they'd mutter, sotto voce, sidling past me in the hallway.

But the adults—Mrs. Warren and her company, who only yesterday had so rigorously endeavored to plumb my motivations—now maintained an elaborate silence, the lid clamped down on the fire in the pan, and never mentioned the incident again.

"Hi, Caroline," they'd cry too brightly in greeting.

"Hello!" I'd smile back cheerily, accomplice to their plan.

Why silence? I'm sure because the subject made everyone hideously uncomfortable. Because to speak of it would only be to give it shape and substance and permanence. Because no one could imagine that something might be seriously amiss with me—scrappy and sturdy and reliable me. You remember the niece in *The Munsters,* the nice perky blond girl who is the wholesomely ordinary note amid the wackiness of her gothic relatives? That was the role to which I appeared to be inseparably wedded: solid and steady Caroline. I always suffered an uneasy suspicion that in the hierarchy of eccentricities that was my extended family, I figured as something of a pedestrian disappointment. Yet I felt an obligation to play my role as it was expected to be performed. I had a responsibility to appear responsible. That's what people were counting on me for. That's who they needed me to be.

There was no way there could be anything really wrong with twelve-year-old me. Puppy love, maybe, or a pimple, or maybe a fight with my sister or a bad grade on a test. "Adolescent angst," my father used to pronounce such matters, and they rated about as high as dust bunnies and soap scum in relation to Life's Big Issues.

How much of the way we end up seeing ourselves is shaped by our own interpretations? When you construct your worldview on a series of misunderstandings, it's like building a skyscraper with the foundation out of plumb: A fractional misalignment at the bottom becomes a whopping divergence from true by the time you get to the top. What that silence meant to me was that I had committed an act so appalling as to be literally unspeakable.

5

In the boarding school's required dress of coat and tie, he managed always, nevertheless, a certain ironic scruffiness, as though condescending to wear the outfit was more an amused indulgence on his part than an actual bow to authority. This boy, this bad-boy sophomore, one of my father's students. He wasn't all that bad, really, just indifferent and unambitious, and at the time that looked like bad to me. I thought it was your obligation always to try harder, and it seemed he wasn't interested in trying at all. He slouched along bored, his tie just this much the wrong side of well-knotted, an incipient shadow of dirty-blond beard sketching the planes of his face, his manner suggesting it was all too much of a bother for him. In the end he'd be just another boy who would never particularly fail and never particularly make much of himself, and didn't particularly care, but when I was twelve that looked reckless and daring.

I was twelve and I lived in a boys' boarding school, and though he was by no means the first of my ardent crushes for the year, for a certain time I believed that all my happiness would lie in the moment when this boy cupped my face in his hands and brushed my lips with his own.

He was fifteen and he was bored and he flirted with me because why not? It filled the empty hours. We traded clumsy double entendres wrapped within fiery exchanges of feigned antagonism.

"You little minx!" he'd cry in pretended outrage, lunging after me as I snatched his wallet from the pocket of his blazer and danced away laughing, eyes wide with excitement at my daring.

Staying just beyond the reach of his hands, I'd pluck through his wallet, my fingers an insinuating intimacy once removed, pull out the driver's learning permit, the Social Security card, the photograph of that other girl, his claimed girlfriend, at another boarding school too far away to seem real—all blond Botticelli rising out of the bland blue sea of the school-portrait backdrop. Her picture made me not jealous so much as strangely exhilarated, like a voyeur.

———————

That spring, on Sunday afternoons in the empty school auditorium, he would draw me behind the heavy, musty drape of the backstage masking curtains, his kisses the pro forma tribute we understood was demanded by the protocol of the occasion in order to license his hands to roam freely about the domain of my flesh.

Those hands, dried and cracked from the winter cold, scratched at my skin. The air smelled thick, textured with the dust from those curtains. I watched motes drift idly through the beam of sunlight falling through the open stage door. *So this is it,* I thought.

It's not that I didn't want to be there—this novel recreation intrigued me; it was uncharted territory. That my body was the ground of this exploration was neither important nor unimportant, really nothing more than a statement of the obvious. It didn't feel as if it had any relevance to me. It didn't particularly feel, even, like my body. It was just a body, and on those afternoons it was a body performing in one particular guise out of the number in which it had been lately appearing.

***

One afternoon he slouched against a wall, arms folded, to engage me in the usual dialogue of innuendo. He shifted position, absent-mindedly shoving up the frayed sleeve of his yellow button-down shirt, revealing on his forearm a series of ugly gashes, dried and crusted. He wanted me to ask.

"What'd you do?" I gasped, riveted by the raw slashes, the blood-rusty stains on his shirt.

"Razor blade." He laughed, dismissive. It was lurid, livid—beneath his notice. Who knew what games he and his friends had been up to, who were always double-daring each other with buck knives and bravado?

I couldn't stop staring. I knew how the skin would feel with the feverish burn of those wounds. Of course, razor blades—why had this never occurred to me before?

***

Razor blades. When I was a kid, I was intrigued by the little slot in the back of the medicine cabinet, the one you could shove a worn razor blade through to dispose of it. Why, I wondered, did razor blades merit their own means of disposal? Why couldn't they go in the trash like everything else? And if you took down a house, ripped out a wall, would you find entombed within it a thousand rusty blades drifted like metallic snow among the joists?

Razor blades. They of the Jekyll-and-Hyde reputation. The razor shaves us for work, for passion, for college interviews and wedding receptions and Sunday visits with the in-laws. Then there is that other razor, the razor of extinguished hope and surrendered expectations, flaying open a wrist like a gutted fish.

But there's another kind of razor, too, for the laying down of edges, the definition of borders.

I started with a Bic disposable razor from the linen closet at home. Cross-legged on my bedroom floor, I fingered the yellow plastic guard over the blade, then pulled it off to brush my fingers lightly over the edge of the blade itself. I broke away the plastic sheath surrounding the razor, and it cracked with a crisp and satisfying snap under the prying blade of my Swiss Army knife. I felt methodical, reasonable, like a home handyman with a project, my tools laid out before me. How clever of me so artfully to dissect this plastic assemblage.

At last the razor—slender, gleaming dully in its plastic bed. I plucked it from its housing, perversely careful not to cut my fingers.

In the utter stillness of the afternoon, the sunlight poured through my window to warm the honey-colored wood of the floor where I sat, amid a scattering of toys from some other lifetime only a few months gone.

I let the razor's edge kiss the pale skin near my left elbow, and then drew it slowly—so slowly that I could feel through the blade the faintest tug of resistance and the sudden giving way of the flesh—along my arm. There was a very fine, an elegant pain, hardly a pain at all, like the swift and fleeting burn of a drop of hot candle wax. In the razor's wake, the skin melted away, parted to show briefly the milky white subcutaneous layers before a thin, beaded line of rich crimson blood seeped through the inch-long divide. Then the blood welled up and began to distort the pure, stark edges of my delicately wrought wound.

The chaos in my head spun itself into a silk of silence. I had distilled myself to the immediacy of hand, blade, blood, flesh.

6

I was twelve, and I lived in a boys' boarding school.

I've gotten almost to expect the raised eyebrow, the intimating smirk, when I tell people where I grew up.

When I was twelve, the odds seemed deliriously in my favor, a fact I attempted to play for some cachet among my own friends from school during the bleary late-night junk-food stupors of slumber parties. We'd be flopped on our patchwork-pattern sleeping bags, and I'd be holding court at center stage, trying to sketch a general image of myself as a woman of worldly expertise, without being pressed too closely on any of the many points about which I was actually still quite vague.

"Of *course* I've kissed a boy like that," I'd say with the world-weariness of a jaded courtesan.

"EEEWW! With tongues?" they'd shriek.

I'd fix them a withering glance, neither confirming nor deny-ing.

When we moved to this boys' boarding school, however, I had only just turned three, and for the next eight years, if I thought of the boys at all, it was only to consider them rather goofy, all arms and legs in a puppyish excess of earnestness and energy. One or two boys in particular might feature as favored baby-sitters, who would come over and entertain my sister and me with ridiculous stories and scrambling, giggling games, and let us write notes in the margins of the letters they were composing to faraway girlfriends. The rest of them—well, they were just the Boys, mere cosmic background noise.

My father was hired in 1965 to come teach English and serve double-duty as chaplain. Or rather, the school needed a chaplain, and in my father they found one who conveniently came with an A.B. in English from Harvard, which is the kind of credential you like to wave in front of parents if you're a boarding school looking to convince them to deliver their sons and unship their checking accounts into your hands.

"This is *it?*" said my mother, aghast, as my father drove us from National Airport outside Washington, along ever-narrower roads, past listing frame houses and decrepit barns and broken-down Chevies propped up on cinder blocks, over rolling hills dotted with scrubby cows, legs and bellies stained orange-red from the Virginia clay. Only my father had scouted our new home before we moved there; we had left the crisply manicured, elm-lined streets of sub-urban Chicago for a rural Virginia county of defeated trailer homes and endemic, hardscrabble poverty at the foot of the Blue Ridge Mountains.

"It's fairly remote," my father had warned my mother, but her idea of "remote" was the farmlands of Vermont, the cabined woods of New England where she'd spent her camp summers.

I think she passed the first few years in Virginia stunned, as though she'd been the butt of an ingeniously complex practical joke and she was still waiting for the punch line, the moment when Allen Funt would emerge from behind the stage set to clap her on the back and commend her for being such a good sport.

Eventually, she became a teacher as well, but she never quite lost that aura of bemusement. "Thirty days hath September . . ." she used to mutter over a scribbled stack of midwinter exam blue books, finishing the old mnemonic with ". . . except in boarding school, where February lasts forever."

In Virginia, we were thirty miles from the nearest town, Charlottesville, a sleepy university burg where people drifted languorously as though the heat of the summers had penetrated to their bones. The miles that separated us from this minor bastion of civilization were paved with narrow, unmarked strips of tar that melted out black, oily bubbles in the summer heat, and always threatened to unveil just around the next bend some thirty-year-old pickup truck barreling down the middle of the road at you and swerving violently only when it seemed it must certainly be too late.

Our mailing address was the one-building town of Dyke, a general store with a post office tacked on the side, perched at the intersection of two roads to nowhere. The store smelled of chewing tobacco and the smoked hams dangling from the rafters, and everything remained perpetually enshrouded in a fine coating of dust, churned up by the trucks that congregated in the parking lot like so many ants about a crumb. Vegetables lay mummified beneath a thick layer of plastic wrap. Hamburger of dubious provenance lurked in the refrigerator case. The proprietor/postmaster slid stamps and small change across the marble countertop with the stumps of fingers severed at the joint slaughtering hogs.

There were always a few locals—as we called them, implicitly suggesting that no matter how long we lived there, we would never be local—hanging around, swapping gossip in a nearly unintelligible dialect and snacking on exotic Southern food like Moon Pies and pork rinds and Yoo-Hoo chocolate sodas. They were sunburned and T-shirted; in youth they were sinewy like rawhide; by their late twenties their wiry frames started to soften and spread, pooling and then cascading over the cinch of their belts.

In the heart of all this, of course, a boys' boarding school—why not? When the board assembled itself with the idea of creating a prep school for boys who, in the words of the school literature, *have had difficulty finding success in the traditional academic setting,* someone knew someone who knew how they might come about acquiring the moldering remains of a now-defunct missionary school. Thus the campus had risen Lazarus-like from its dead self, though when we moved there it was still considerably more dead than risen. The buildings crumbled around us, holes gaped in the ceilings, plaster sifted down in little flurries, floorboards gave way. What I remember most, however, about those earliest years was that the walls of whatever residence we occupied fairly seethed with the fluttering and buzzing and scurrying of legions of birds, bees, flies, bats. Our Siamese cat used to sit in my bedroom window in one house, crunching dead flies like popcorn.

We were housed in first one, then another of these decrepit buildings, the headmaster shuffling the faculty about like an endless game of three-card monte, but gradually the school's finances gained ground and the worst of the old structures toppled at the nudge of a wrecking ball. When I was nine we were granted occupancy of a gloriously spanking-new four-bedroom brick house, complete with the decadent luxuries of thunderous water pressure and level, unsplintered floors, and doors that slipped neatly into plumb frames.

The campus itself was impossibly beautiful, nestled in an elbow of the Blue Ridge, with the mountains rising behind our backs and the Piedmont rolling away in front of us. The thousand acres of the campus were a sheltered enclave, the shack-and-trailer ambiance of the surrounding county invisible to us there.

I thought surely God must be an academic—didn't time slip perfectly into the alternating rhythms of school and vacation? Could there be any more perfect life than to live on this campus, with a pool and a gymnasium and two lakes, canoes in summer and ice skating in winter, trees made for climbing and streams for wading, and always the mountains unveiling something new every season?

Mine was the best of all possible lives, and though I knew it was nothing like the lives led by my own classmates, its uniqueness served only to underline my good fortune. I felt grievous pity for those classmates from school, in distant Charlottesville, hemmed in by sidewalks and backyard fences and streets they couldn't cross alone.

In the winter, the wind poured down off the mountains in a roaring rush of ten thousand bare trees scratching at the sky, a sound that made my own warm bed, with its gathered retinue of stuffed animals and sleeping cats, the very essence of luxurious abundance.

In spring, green would explode in a lush profusion of mountain laurel and honeysuckle and dense tangles of Virginia creeper that misted their way slowly up the slopes of the mountains. My father would gather up my sister and me and a handful of boys and the tents smelling of mildew from a winter shelved in the basement, and we'd all go camping in the Shenandoah National Forest, scooping up greasy Hamburger Helper by the light of a Coleman lantern.

Then spring would decline into summer with the languor of a screen ingenue swooning into a chaise longue. In June and August my family decamped to the Eastern Shore of Virginia for the long school vacation. In July summer school was in session, and my sister and I passed the blanketing heat of those summer days submerged in the school's pool like crocodiles in a chlorinated pond, surfacing only to sun on the cement deck until our mother rounded us up for meals. In the thick stillness of summer evenings, the steady thrum of the bullfrogs in the lake mixed in strange harmony with the whir of cicadas and the soprano chirrup of tree peepers, until the air was textured with the sound.

In the fall, the boys would come back. The Mercedeses and the Volvos and the Lincolns emerged one after the other in regal procession through the stone gates that marked the campus entrance. Trunks were unloaded, blazers brought forth from the dry cleaner's wrap in which they'd spent the summer entombed, radios started blaring out newly reopened dormitory windows, the smell of succotash and Tater Tots drifted from the school kitchen's exhaust fans. The rhythm of our lives began over again.

We lived by the boys' schedule, our waking hours punctuated by the chattering metallic ring of the alarm bells that divided the days into minutely scheduled interludes. From 6:00 A.M. Wake-up to 10:10 P.M. Lights Out (an indulgent 11:10 on Saturday nights), the bells signaled the day's transitions, from bed to breakfast to chapel to classes to athletics to supper to study hall to bed.

This painstaking structuring of the boys' lives was part of the school's strategy to rescue its charges from histories of academic failure. The boys were not disciplinary cases, but rather the dyslexic, the too easily distracted, and only occasionally the simply dumb. Here at the foot of the Blue Ridge they were removed from girls, parties, cars, movies, and all the other little teenage hazards by means of which a boy with only half a mind to his studies might trip and founder. For entertainment, they were offered a weekly trip into somnolent Charlottesville, and a Saturday night movie screened in the school auditorium—B-grade monster flicks and cheesy Westerns or whatever could be rented cheap from the distributor.

We ate all our meals with the boys in the echoing barn of the school dining room, with a student's painting of the school's emblem—St. George slaying the dragon—mounted over the baronial stone fireplace at one end and gradually, over the years, bespattered with malicious shots of ketchup, butter pats, and even, I remember, one desiccated olive still flying its forlorn pimiento flag. The faculty congregated at maybe half a dozen tables, and the boys commandeered the rest. Like any school cafeteria, ours was loud with cutlery and scraping chairs and conversation at volumes sufficient to reach the length of the long wooden tables, all those masculine voices blending to a rumbling bass note.

Inevitably, at every meal, some boy would come up to stand diffidently behind my father's chair.

"Sir, is it too late to sign up for the caving trip?"

"Sir, can we talk about my grade on the test?"

"Sir, my mom wants me to ask you to call her about my college applications."

At every entreaty, my father would turn, still with fork in hand, perhaps chewing the last bit of toast or lettuce, to offer his full attention.

As faculty, we had the dubious privilege of cutting ahead of the boys in the cafeteria line, where we shuffled along, meekly accepting the plates like some country-fried Communion thrust toward us by the kitchen help. We dined off fiberglass trays, using industrial-grade stainless-steel utensils; sometimes an unappetizing bit of crusted egg or spinach clung still to a fork or knife.

Those meals were all resolutely rural Southern: eggs and sausages and fried apples and pancakes and grits all composed upon a foundation of bacon grease; vegetables boiled into submission and dotted with gelatinous globs of ham fat; meatish things congealed in a pool of gravy; canned fruit salad snowed under by sweetened coconut; bread pudding, collard greens, squat cubes of cake cut from yard-long baking trays and smeared with a thin film of frosting in pink or white or yellow. In the unlikely event you might want seconds, you couldn't have them anyway.

At the end of each meal our trays were drawn away into the steaming bowels of the kitchen by means of a stained and yellowed rubber conveyor belt, like so many boats making their funeral procession across a River Styx smelling always ever so vaguely of sour milk.

Because we so rarely ate at home, our own kitchen was the least-used room in our house, its cupboards mostly bare but for some instant coffee and a few packets of mix 'n' serve oatmeal, the refrigerator home to little more than an ancient tub of margarine and a bottle of martini olives. On vacations our expeditions to the Safeway in Charlottesville were fantastical adventures; I roamed the aisles in wonderment at the exotic possibilities of Tuna Helper, SpaghettiOs, Swanson's frozen dinners.

"Kraft Mac-a-Chee!" my sister and I clamored. "Spaghetti!"

These were the ultimate symbols of our brief paroles from institutional dining, and to this day they conjure up for me the taste of liberation.

On vacations my mother used to try to approximate something like normal family life, but the rest of my family were like the congenitally blind suddenly given sight and unable to make sense of the shapes, patterns, and colors of ordinary domestic life before us. My mother would struggle to get us all to sit down together at the dinner table. She'd explain to my sister and me the difference between a salad fork and a dinner fork, and the fine art of the butter knife, for the day when we might be confronted with a meal that wasn't served up on a tray with a paper napkin. Then my father would induce anarchy by alleging that you could tell crystal from glass by wetting your finger and drawing it around the rim of a wine goblet until it begins to hum. The next thing you knew, we'd all be dipping our fingers and setting our glass rims humming.

But for my mother's stubborn insistence, the rest of us would have sat happily through every meal each with a book propped up in front of our plates, and in spite of her best efforts there were still a lot of sauce- or jelly-stained books in our house. In our family, someone was always sprawled somewhere with a book. It was that kind of home, sprawling and slouchy and easy. We all wore plastic ponchos from K-Mart when it rained, and carried our clothes in backpacks when we traveled.

When I visited my school friends in their homes—a relatively rare occurrence, made complicated by the distance between us—I felt like some anthropologist among the native peoples, taking my mental field notes: *Ah, so this is how they live.*

I assumed that every one of these homes was completely representative of the rest. They had living rooms we kids (meant to confine ourselves to finished basements equipped with bean-bag chairs and console TVs) entered as if making an illegal border crossing, tiptoeing across impossibly white carpeting, threading our way cautiously through furniture as stiff and formal as an etiquette lesson, oppressed by the hushed, lifeless atmosphere of a mausoleum. These homes had kitchens straining at the seams with a gluttonous plenty of milk and vegetables and sodas and brightly colored packages of Ho-Hos and Cheez Doodles and crinkly cellophane bags of egg noodles. The dads wore aprons that said "Chief Cook and Bottle Washer," and they grilled burgers and hot dogs on backyard barbecues. The moms made deviled eggs and Betty Crocker brownies, and around the family dinner table every clink of silver on china rang deafeningly as the father inquired politely about our day, and the kids said, "Yes, sir" and "No, ma'am," and the mother passed chunky bowls of real mashed potatoes and still-recognizable vegetables.

———

My father, only half facetiously, proclaimed everything slopped up to us from the vast vats of the boarding-school kitchen "food of the gods," but the rest of my family poked fun at the food, which we commended to the broad realm of things we classified as "Southern," by which we meant the amusingly colorful and incomprehensible manners of a foreign land. Like bitter collard greens studded with pale floes of fat. Like those ancient, dusty pickup trucks. Like the women of a certain age who had their hair "done" once a week into stiff, unyielding, impossibly vertical masses of curls, and exclaimed, "Oh mah Lawd!" at the least remarkable bit of news, holding an alarmist hand to the chest as though warding off a heart attack.

Once again, we were in a place but not of it. We thought of ourselves as Yankees, expatriates of a lost homeland, the North, which I vaguely idealized as an urbane bastion of sophisticated pleasures and enlightened ideologies. This North was not quite the same as the actual North I experienced when we visited our relatives in Boston and upstate New York; that North was a place of sooty snow and abrasive accents that I could never wait to get back to Virginia from. And yet I continued to think of myself as a Northerner, until I went off to college in one of those quintessential New England college towns marked by diehard liberalism and the pointed spire of the Congregational church. At which point I began to think of myself as a Southerner, defending my home against the cumulative clichés wrought by *Gone With the Wind, Deliverance,* and *The Dukes of Hazzard.*

Except, "You're from the South," people would say to me suspiciously, then: "Where's your accent?"

I sometimes think not belonging, in my family, is in our bones.

7

When the boys stopped being for me simply the Boys, generic, it happened as swiftly and suddenly as the fall of a guillotine, severing my life entirely from what it had been.

On one of those almost painfully clear early fall afternoons when the warmth of the day is undercut with the slightest edge of the autumn chill to come, I wandered across campus, ambling along on some dreaming twelve-year-old's mission. Some boys were playing touch football in the field overlooking the gymnasium, scrambling and shouting in what always struck me as the pointless chaos of a stupid game.

The ball slipped through someone's hands and bounced, in that drunken, wobbling way of footballs, nearly to my feet.

"Hey," said one of the boys, panting up next to me to retrieve the ball, "wanna play?"

If over the years the boys had mostly made no specific impression on me, I suppose I had likewise made little impression on most of them. Faculty kid. Maybe on a long hiking trip one of them might carry me on his shoulders, or after dinner some night a few of them might josh around with me, teasing me, or toss a Frisbee with me and my sister. So it was neither ordinary nor extraordinary that this boy would invite me to play.

But "No," I said. "I hate football."

"What!" he exclaimed, pausing in the act of scooping the ball up from the ground. "How can you hate football?"

He was dark-haired, dark-eyed, sinuous in a way I couldn't quite define. I didn't know his name.

"It's stupid," I said. "It's boring. Nothing ever happens. It's twenty seconds of running around and jumping on each other and then everyone stands around for the next five minutes."

"How can you hate football? It's the Great American Sport!"

"Yeah, well, I still hate it."

My teachers were always writing on my report cards comments like *very forceful in her opinions; very independent and reluctant to take advice; strong-minded; strong-willed;* and *not afraid to raise conflicting opinions.* I had opinions, and I defended them like a terrier with a bone. I hated football. There was no compromising.

"Come on, try it. Just once," said the dark-haired boy, whom I would come to know as equally stubborn and argumentative.

By now the rest of the boys, maybe six or seven of them, had drifted over. They stood around us, laughing, amused at this standoff.

"I don't have to try it. I know I hate it. I hate it on TV. I hate it at school."

"Look, you have to try it once," said the dark-haired boy, standing squarely before me, one hand on his hip, the other cradling the ball. "You don't get tackled," he said patiently. "You just run around with the ball. It's fun. How can you not want to play touch football? *Everyone* plays touch football."

"I've never played it. I think it's stupid."

"Aaargh!" he said, raising the ball up in mock frustration, turning to his compatriots as though for reinforcement.

"You might as well try it," laughed one of the other boys, blond, in glasses and a faded red short-sleeved sweatshirt. "He always gets what he wants," he said.

I fell for it, thinking they were mounting some serious effort to convince me to like touch football; I was going to prove just how obstinate I could be by not liking it anyway. Instead, they tossed me the ball and then all of them instantly converged on me, dragging me into a group tackle, a harmless tumble of bodies on the damp October ground. Just the kind of teasing joke you would pull on somebody's kid sister, but for me the world changed key— only the slightest shift in tone that would make all the difference. The feel of those strong arms wrapped around me branded my flesh.

———

After that afternoon, I'd find myself drifting with deliberate nonchalance after dinner toward the lobby outside the dining room, where my sister, fourteen, gathered a nightly audience of suppliants. This lobby was really a reception area bordering the administrative offices, where current or prospective students' families might wait before meeting the headmaster, the admissions director. It was carpeted, with sofas and wingback chairs upholstered in the loud yellows and oranges of the seventies, and recent-vintage yearbooks on the coffee tables, and oil-painted likenesses of benefactors blandly overseeing all.

Wandering by, I'd imagine that I gave the impression it was mere coincidence, that I was just passing through the lobby on my way to other, important and pressing matters. But oh, what a surprise! Here was Mike or James or Robert, one of the same boys I had met on that football afternoon, and I supposed I might stop just for a moment, even though of course I had those other important matters to attend to.

Unlike my wretched classmates at school, these were the kind of boys you could dream of, with deep voices and easy, ropy young men's bodies and the simple superiority of their age—fifteen, sixteen, seventeen years old—bespeaking sophistications I could only half imagine. How could I have failed to notice them all these years? I wondered.

They still hardly noticed me. They came to the lobby in search of my sister. She had a sweeping, imperious manner and a blanket disdain for the lot of them that made all those boys mad for her. She could hardly step outside the dining room door before she gathered a retinue, boys materializing almost from thin air to circle her like so many electrons around an atom. We'd all laughed about it the summer before, how my sister had to make a mad dash through the thicket of boys, like a movie star wading through her adoring fans. The more she avoided them, the more they pursued. She had center stage, whether she wanted it or not.

She had chosen, however, a boyfriend, a senior no less, who could see the light from my sister's window from his dorm room at night. The nature of their relationship, in that context, was hopelessly unusual. They never had a date. During his few free hours—the school was miserly in granting these—he could come and sit on our porch, or she could go sit on the fence with him in front of his dorm.

From my perspective, it seemed as if they were perpetually in the throes of some highly charged emotional confrontation just out of my earshot, she gesticulating angrily, he shaking his head, and the sound of their voices drifting faint and unintelligible to me. I thought this must be the mark of a Serious Relationship. I assumed these confrontations were fraught with great meaning and import.

Her boyfriend used to enlist me as envoy after their fights, my job to plead his case and argue his merits. I felt very grown-up and important to be made privy to such rarefied matters.

"Tell your sister, God, I just love her, and she's, she's making me crazy," he'd say, and when he said this his face would tighten up in a grimace as though his suffering caused him actual, physical pain, and I could see how desire and torment were bound up together in his need for her and I thought, *No one will ever love me like that.*

My sister's life seemed like the most glamorous thing in the world. She was in ninth grade in the big, cheerleaders-and-football-team-and-pep-rallies public high in Charlottesville, with exotic acronyms instead of boring old homeroom and lunch: **T**eacher **A**dvisory **P**eriod and **L**unch **A**ctivity **P**eriod. I couldn't imagine that she had ever suffered a moment of gawky, giggly pubescence; we had been children together, and then one day I found I had been left behind and she had rematerialized, wholly realized, as this coolly sophisticated creature who wrote her journal in French and deigned to submit to the ardent entreaties of her lover as a queen might bestow a touch of her hand upon a grateful subject.

When my sister hung out in the lobby after dinner, with her boyfriend and his friends, a small crowd inevitably coalesced with her at its center. And there I'd be, excited and bewildered and milling around the edge of things like the family mutt—everyone pats you absentmindedly on the head but no one takes particular notice of you.

Here my sister was reaping the whole teenager swag and booty, just by virtue of being born two years ahead of me. Not for the first time, I reflected on the injustice of always getting stuck in what amounted to the understudy's role by the blind misfortune of birth order. I was doomed, I thought, always to be the little kid hanging on the periphery. I felt as though my twelveness announced itself in every detail, in my blue jeans gathered and belted to scrawny, boyish hips, in the perpetual tattoo of black and purple felt tip on my hands from notes and reminders I'd written to myself, in my waist-length tangle of hair, which I only intermittently remembered to address.

Twelve was such an in-between age, too old to be excused on the basis of youth, too young to be allowed the privileges of age. Still sitting at the children's table on holidays, but expected to set an example for the younger kids. Twelve sounded like a little kid's age, a footed-pajamas and in-bed-by-nine-o'clock age. I longed to be thirteen, to have that magical "teen" tacked to the end of my age that would grant me access to . . . well . . . I didn't know quite what. But something I was certain I was missing now.

After I'd considered the problem of the long months remaining until my thirteenth birthday the following summer, I began arguing that fall—to anyone who would listen, but most particularly to those boys—that I wasn't really twelve at all.

"I'm really already thirteen," I said. "Because you have to count those nine months when you're alive but just aren't born yet."

I thought perhaps I could exempt myself from twelve by sheer force of argument. If I were thirteen, officially "teen," then wouldn't those boys come to the lobby in search of me as well?

8

Ensconced in the bathroom at home, where I could scrub it all guiltily away almost as soon as I'd applied it, I dabbed on my wrists my mother's Love's Lemon Fresh scent, I smeared on my eyelids pollen-green shadow left over from my chorus role in last year's school musical. With a disposable razor spirited from the linen closet, I shaved my legs, rushing, expecting at any moment to be apprehended in that compromising position, so that the razor jumped and skittered up my shinbone to leave a little hopscotch of bleeding nicks. I wrapped the disposable carefully in the fold of my towel and when no one was looking thrust it into the far depths of the closet again, where no one would find it used and suspect me.

My relationship with girlness was tortured. "You do that like a girl," my sister and I might sling at each other as the lowest sort of insult. Girlness I'd always considered a contemptible amalgam of ruffled curtains and Barbie's Dream House and those ridiculous underwear with the days of the week embroidered on them. Girlness was mincing and squealing.

Being a girl in the strictly biological sense, however, did not necessarily condemn you to girlness, so long as you remained unrepentantly scabby and exercised the proper vigilance against lace-trimmed ankle socks and dotting your i's with little hearts. Yet I suffered furtive fascinations with alien girlness. When I was six, seven years old I used to linger over the pink ballerina costume in the Sears catalog, wondering with delicious horror what it would be like to prance about in that stiff tulle skirt and those silken slippers. As the salesman at the shoe store fitted me with yet another pair of stolid, serviceable Buster Browns, I glanced surreptitiously at the glossy black patent-leather party shoes I would never in a zillion, trillion years consent to wear but, oh, if I could just try them on, just once. I would never, however, have admitted to such shameful yearnings. I begged for a doll for my eighth Christmas— an ordinary baby doll—but when she came to me, crystal-blue-eyed and propped up in a pink plastic baby seat behind the cellophane window of her box, I was so ashamed of her that when I took her to play at someone else's house, I would smuggle her there in an anonymous brown paper bag, scurrying along in dread of the possibility that someone would stop and ask me what I had in the bag.

I'm not sure precisely how I'd formed such a low opinion of girlness, except that I lived, of course, in the Boy Center of the Universe. What's more, in my favorite books it was always the boys who had adventures in the wilderness and pursued mythic quests and poled their rafts down the mighty Mississippi, while the girls got stuck making sandwiches and running for help. Who'd want to be the girl?

What a cruel fate, then, to find myself at twelve suddenly in desperate want of a crash course in girlness. It seemed to me that an easy mastery of the art of being a girl was the necessary precursor to elevating myself to that rarefied Olympian status of being, like my sister, someone's Girlfriend. Girlfriends were personified, in my mind, by the mascaraed and miniskirted girls who arrived by the busload from St. Margaret's and Madeira and Foxcroft for school dances. Their hair bounced and swirled like a shampoo commercial. They could do that girl business of leaning forward and glancing up shyly winsome from under a silky cascade of bangs—a trick that would, a few years later, become the trademarked Princess Diana look. They gave off exotic scents and clustered giggling in the bathroom with a mysterious array of implements spread out on the chrome shelves over the sinks—wands and brushes and puffs—with which they dabbed at eyelashes and cheeks and lips. The evidence of their passage remained behind in powdery residues and crumpled tissues imprinted with lipsticked kisses.

I felt like I was way behind the loop in this girl business, with no possible hope of catching up. How did other girls seem so natural, so easy in their girlness? When, at my mother's insistence, I wore my first bra, I felt as awkward as if I'd been strapped into a suit of armor. I felt sure everyone in the world would know. Attention would be called. Great hilarity enjoyed at my expense.

This same apprehension met my every furtive flirtation with makeup, powders, perfumes, the whole girl paraphernalia. I just knew I would be the subject of endless mockery and derision if anyone caught wise to what I was up to.

Apparently I'd been such a reluctant recruit to my own sex that I wasn't invited the day they took the other girls aside and explained to them how the whole girl business worked. Not the nuts-and-bolts stuff with body parts that you learn in health class. No, this was some secret conventicle in the girls' hut where they anointed the postulants with body splash and went over the essential ground rules: how to make yourself comfortable in your girl self, how to use eyeliner or wander into the lingerie department without feeling like an impostor who at any moment might be unmasked and denounced.

9

When an avalanche is on the very verge of breaking away, the weight of a single footfall can set it in motion. A boy says to you one night, there in the lobby, "I was hoping you'd show up," and something shoots through you hot, fizzing, dizzying.

Then I was on the inside, just like that, as though I'd slipped through Alice's mirror. There were boys who plopped down next to me in the lobby, boys who after breakfast, before I left for school, would lean against a doorjamb talking just to me, their books slung under their arms.

I can't tell you why any of them ever gave me a second look. Out of boredom, maybe. To amuse themselves? It would be easy to say that they were manipulating the situation, manipulating *me* to their advantage, but the most inexplicable thing of all is that I think they were, in their own way, sincere. I have still the letters they wrote me, and today their words seem almost pathetically earnest: *I will never, ever forget you, not as long as I live.*

There is no other time in your life when just sitting around in idle, pointless conversation will feel so fabulously significant as it does when you are twelve, fifteen, sixteen; hanging out is the consuming passion of adolescence. Sometimes we'd cram, two or three of us, into the narrow box of the projection booth in the auditorium, full of empty movie-reel canisters and misplaced notebooks and random lengths of discarded patching film, while one of my coterie served as projectionist of the Saturday evening movie. I felt important just to *be* there, in an inner sanctum of cool, tipped back on two legs of a stool with the rough cinder-block wall against my shoulders and the noisy clattering of the film spooling through the projector.

Mostly, however we sprawled together in that lobby, arguing, bantering, shouting, remonstrating, all of the talk shot through with subtext and suggestion. It was an orgy of insinuations, an erotica of implications.

I can't remember now anything of what we said, but I can remember the feeling of those highly charged interludes. There was something powerful and narcotic and forbidden throbbing just below the surface of our conversations, the way a glimpse of naked skin is so much more seductive than a body simply laid bare. If a faculty member walked by, we'd all fall into sudden silence.

Out of a frequently fluctuating assembly there in the lobby grew a tight, intricate entanglement of only four of us: me, that dark-eyed boy with the football, his roommate the blond boy from that same afternoon, and that other one, the scofflaw, the rebel of indifference.

At first it was all talk. Then it was letters scribbled feverishly during the long, dull school hours that separated us. Letters we folded into tight squares and thrust surreptitiously into each other's hands after a quick glance about for the disapproving glare of any faculty, like spies effecting any information exchange.

Letters alternating long plaints of school-induced boredom with sudden declarations of passion and pragmatic discussions of opportunities we might steal to be thrown into each other's company.

Then there was an afternoon when they told me they would teach me how to kiss.

"You gotta know how to do it right," they said.

"Okay," I said, feeling a low trill of daring curl through me, co-conspirator, willing accomplice. And then they kissed me one after the other, spinning me in a circle of hands, arms, lips, tongues. Oh it was intoxicating, heady, delirious, as though I had suddenly discovered just at the edge of my grasp a world of vertiginous excitements I could never have imagined existed.

"There's a lot more I could show you," said the dark-haired boy on another afternoon.

I knew it was mere speculative boasting—throw it up against the wall and see what sticks. I knew, and what's more he knew that I knew, but that was part of the game; you had to burst out of the gate with all your colors flying and brazen your way through on sheer bravado.

"Oh yeah?" I said, and I managed to convey in my reply both skepticism and challenge, as though to suggest that there wasn't one damn thing he could show me that I hadn't already mastered and put behind me.

That was the pose I struck, jaded worldliness, though half the time I didn't even know what was being talked about. Whom would I have asked for a translation?

I thought I was just playing rather cleverly at an exciting game, dancing along a step ahead of the implications and the innuendoes. Nothing else interested me but those brief, dizzying moments in their company. When we were apart, I filled the hours in dreamy reverie. I tried to imagine the boys imagining me. Did they lie in their beds at night staring at the ceiling, as I did, replaying every word of the day's conversation? Did they daydream of me during class? Did they talk about me together in their dorm rooms? In these hours by myself I colored reality freely with shades of fantasy, imagining something along the lines of Zeffirelli's *Romeo and Juliet*—blank verse and giddy passions and a boy who'd be willing to die for the love of me.

We had maybe half an hour after dinner on weeknights, a few hours here and there on weekends, but even when we were apart I could feel their presence like a constant whisper. They were there, somewhere, and anytime I left my house they might see me. I imagined, even, that the boys might glance a thousand yards across the lake and see me in my bedroom, so every time I crossed in front of the window, it was like stepping onto a proscenium stage, me thinking, *Now they will see me brushing my hair, so I must brush my hair as women do in movies, lingering and dreamy.* Sometimes I crouched low beneath the level of the windowsill, to play secretively with my toys.

Self-consciousness crept over me like an itch, making its way into my skin, my pores, my blood, my bones; everywhere I went on campus I felt like I was appearing in performance as the Object of Desire. Her stage directions were not fully clear to me, but I patched together her character from the odds and ends of my experience: TV romances and the trashy novels circulated surreptitiously through the B[1], my sister, all those mixer dance girls I'd watch come and go on Saturday nights over the years. She had to be coy and ironic, worldly and flirtatious, clever and coolly sophisticated, apparently indifferent to their attentions.

The most agonizing and yet thrilling of my daily appearances was nightly supper in the dining hall. My sister swept through the heavy, swinging wooden doors at the entrance, the great roiling current of her passage almost visible to me. I scuttled behind in her wake, into the glare of an imagined spotlight in which each of my moves was a closely observed performance as I picked up my tray, moved through the line, reached for silverware, filled a glass with milk. Oh God, what if I dropped a glass or my tray, spilled ketchup or gravy on my shirt, left a morsel of cottage cheese nestled in the corner where top lip meets bottom?

The essential feature of the performance was that each elaborately stagy move—talking with my sister, laughing at a joke, biting into an apple—had to be carried out with no apparent self-consciousness. I had to *appear* blithely unaware. Act natural. I never dared look directly at any of the boys I knew, for fear of catching them in the act of watching me, and thereby acknowledging my part in the performance.

I have no evidence to prove anyone actually *was* watching me, but I imagined they were, and in the end there is no difference between the two. I could feel the strain like winter ice on the verge of breaking up, the hiss of fracture lines snaking across my nights as I sat alone in my bedroom, oddly desolate and unable to pinpoint why.

10

By the time my parents understood the situation that had developed, it was already too late.

"I don't want you spending so much time with them," said my mother. "They're too old. It's inappropriate."

What did she mean, "inappropriate"?

"But they're my friends!" I protested, frustrated that she seemed determined not to understand.

"They aren't your friends. They're too old to be your friends."

What a ridiculous thing for her to say, I thought. Why was she being so unreasonable? Of course they were my friends. Didn't they seek me out after dinner, on weekend afternoons? Didn't their letters say *I hope I will see you tonight*?

From my mother's point of view, the whole situation was no doubt alarmingly clear, but to explore its implications and ramifications would have required of both of us a language of the uncomfortable that neither of us knew how to speak. She couldn't have explained that she was only trying to protect me, and certainly I wouldn't have been likely to hear her. I would have refused to believe then that a day would come when I would regret this too-early plunge into the Byzantine complications of desire. From where I stood, my mother's effort to protect looked more like a cage in the making, and I the offender to be made prisoner therein.

I couldn't quite see the crime in what I was doing, yet it was obvious that the grown-ups disapproved—not just my parents, but other faculty as well, who would pass our little conclaves in the lobby with a scowl of censure. Clearly I wasn't supposed to like these boys, and not being able—not wanting, really—to help myself, I concluded that my feelings themselves must be my transgression, some sort of character flaw that a better person would have done her best to downplay and overcome.

In spite of my stubbornly contentious streak, I'd never been a troublemaker. I sought approval, I coveted it. I liked being a rule-abider, an upholder of standards, a champion of integrity. So the burden of this official disapproval weighed heavily on me as I skulked off to the lobby after dinner, to the movie on Saturday night. Yet the alternative was equally untenable; the company of those boys was like heroin, a rush so intense I had to have more and more of it. What dictate of my heart should I follow? Which preference should gain ascendancy over my heart?

The situation stumped me, and I kept my illicit, outlaw feelings to myself while I tried to puzzle out the proper answer, when no answer appeared to offer itself.

It would never have occurred to me to seek out other counsel, to find someone else I might confide in. Such a notion was beyond the realm of my experience of the world, as inconceivable as reciting the Gettysburg Address in flawless Russian—I wouldn't have had the faintest idea how to do it. It was the natural order of being that you figured things out on your own.

What worried me was that I didn't seem to be coming to the right conclusions. I couldn't seem to come to any conclusions at all, but rather just kept stumbling along blindly, trying to stave off some looming, inevitable disaster.

As though mounting some kind of manic diversionary tactic, I continuously shaped and reshaped and effaced myself to appear in the guise I thought the situation demanded, orchestrating various Carolines for my parents, for the boys, for my administrators at school. I'd long had a habit—no doubt from the influence of so much reading—of imagining myself in the third person. When I was a little kid, this narrative tendency had applied itself mostly to my games:

. . . her breath ragged in her throat, she pressed herself deeper into the shadow of the trees, hoping to avoid her pursuers.

. . . "Well, thank you, Merv, it's certainly a pleasure to be with you here on the show today."

. . . dragging her shattered leg behind her, she inched her way painfully through the mud, knowing everyone's survival depended on her.

Now this manner of regarding my life from a distance, as though I were a character in a performance, had begun to pervade my every transaction with the world. Every word and gesture, even sometimes when I was alone, started to feel more like a theatrical enterprise than anything real. I no longer experienced things so much as I experienced them *as* experiences, a step removed. I played my part, and though the emotions of this character were powerful and vivid and sometimes even overwhelming, still they unfolded at that remove. Over it all, a dry, dispassionate Narrator rambled its observations in the background like the voice-over on a 1950s grade-school science film:

Now he is kissing you, and your fingers brush his arm. . . . Now you are raising your hand in class. . . . Now you are walking along by the lake, and the wind is gently lifting your hair. . . . I could almost hear the faint strains of theme music.

After a while, how do you know what is honestly your own anymore, and not just a fabrication for the sake of the audience?

It was a troubling disembodiment, like a near-death experience in which you can see your self, and everyone around you talking, but you are no longer connected to that self. There was this Caroline, operating in the world, and though I could not detach myself from her entirely, neither could I rejoin her. Every day I got up and went to school, ate my meals, did my homework, walked and talked through my life, but every day I felt I was spinning a little bit further out of my own control, as if I had only the most tenuous connection with that Caroline.

Was it this dissociation that caused me a terrible, itching, twitching restless unease, like the too-familiar hug from a relative I didn't care for? Or was it the classic, irresolvable conflict between desire and duty that left me so anxious, so weighed down with dread? Or was it just my mind itself, coming undone of its own accord, on its own preordained schedule, drowning all my thoughts in a sea of static like the background crackle of an overseas telephone call, where a thousand frantic conversations are carried on just beyond the edge of intelligibility?

It felt physical, this oppressive tension, like something crawling on my flesh, and I wanted to shake it from my skin the way a horse shakes flies. I sat on my bed, digging my fingernails into my face, wanting to tear the skin away. What do you do with a want like that?

In the woods behind my house, on a still winter morning, I smashed a bottle on a rock, a green ginger ale bottle, holding it by the neck with both hands and bringing it down against the smooth face of weathered stone like an ax, a baseball bat, a club. It shattered in a rain of green shards and the fragmented chord of breaking glass, and right in that instant of its shattering came a flash of some release, like a brief rush of cool, fresh air into drowning lungs. Then it was gone again, and I was left with a scattered field of debris and a wash of self-recrimination for the excess of the gesture. I gathered the glass in a sudden worry that one of our cats would step on it and be injured. Then I slunk in the kitchen door with the chunks and slivers of bright green glass heaped in a pouch made by folding the hem of my sweatshirt up to my chest, and buried the evidence of my crime under a layer of garbage in the can.

At night, I danced wildly around in my room in darkness lit only by the yellow glow from the family's old console stereo, which

I'd commandeered for my bedroom, the cheap needle scratching out "Helter Skelter" until my father banged on my closed door, demanding, "Do you have to play that music so loud?"

One Sunday afternoon, my mother stunned me with the casual announcement at lunch that we would all be heading into Charlottesville for the rest of the day to visit with family friends. When I HAD OTHER PLANS! Plans I wasn't supposed to have, of course—since they involved time spent in the company of boys I was expected to be spending less time with—and therefore plans that I couldn't raise as an objection and counterpoint to my mother's.

I sat at the table, staring hatefully at the roast beef and gravy on my plate, deaf to the dining room's clatter of cutlery and rumble of voices and the *whap-whap* of the swinging wooden exit doors, hearing only my own frantic dismay. This was the final outrage, I thought. *I can't bear it.*

I bolted out of the dining room, banging through the swinging doors, even as my Narrator was counseling, *This is stupid. What do you think this is going to do for you?* I ran all the way down the academic building's hall, and shoved through the door, and ran across the lawn, and onto the road that crossed the campus, past the lake, my lungs burning, jumped a fence, cut across a field, raced up the driveway past our house, my feet slipping in the loose gravel. I ran into the woods, slapping at thin branches, my Narrator jollying along going, *Well, my goodness, a runaway scene, and what are you going to do now, stay away forever?*

I already felt stupid. What *was* I going to do now? I could see that I was just going to end up plodding embarrassed out of the woods in some utter anticlimax.

I threw myself down on my back on the forest floor, still gasping for breath. The damp and the chill crept through the thin flannel of my shirt, and I lay there wondering if there was some way simply never to get up, to lie there until the thin winter air and the wet leaves beneath me had emptied me of all concern, all caring.

Somewhere over the course of that winter I started thinking about killing myself, though not so much because I wanted to be dead, precisely, as because I yearned for resolution, for escape from the scratching distress of now. I thought killing myself was the only way I'd get that. Somehow, I wasn't really picturing the long-term consequences of dead: that I'd be dead now, dead later, and dead ad infinitum. I was looking for dead in the short term. Dead until maybe, say, it was time to go to college.

Would I really have killed myself? I don't know. I was skeptical enough even then about my theatrical streak to suspect that suicide might be just another piece in the performance. Slit your wrists in the bathtub, where the warm water makes it easier, I'd heard. The plinking drip from the faucet. The billow of red clouding the water against the bone white of the tub. I could see it all just a little too cinematically, a movie starring the soon-to-be tragically regretted third-person Caroline.

I needed to kill something *in* me, this awful feeling like worms tunneling along my nerves. So when I discovered the razor blade, cutting, if you'll believe me, was my gesture of hope. That first time, when I was twelve, was like some kind of miracle, a revelation. The blade slipped easily, painlessly through my skin, like a hot knife through butter. As swift and pure as a stroke of lightning, it wrought an absolute and pristine division between before and after. All the chaos, the sound and fury, the uncertainty and confusion and despair—all of it evaporated in an instant, and I was for that moment grounded, coherent, whole. *Here is the irreducible self.* I drew the line in the sand, marked my body as mine, its flesh and its blood under my command.

/ /

Why? That's the question you always come back to, the tough one. Why cut? Why, of all things, take a razor blade to my skin?

This is a story about how an ordinary sort of person can end up traveling some dark and unexpected roads. So I can tell you that any one of us might sometimes be driven by blind, inchoate need. I can tell you that the idea and the urge to cut seemed to arise from my very skin itself. That doesn't really answer the question, though.

I can tell you that a well-timed wound focuses the mind marvelously—don't you remember the sudden clarity that followed a skinned knee, a split lip, when all the world came down to body and blood, nerve endings and adrenaline?

I can tell you that on a global human scale, ritualized self-mutilation is surprisingly common. What in Western culture is pathologized as an indicator of profound dysfunction is in other cultures the very vehicle, the visible sign of a society's claim upon that body—in scarification, in tattoos, and in measures more drastic than anything I ever considered.

None of this, of course, answers the question.

I can tell you that our bodies sometimes serve as the symbolic ground where order and disorder fight for supremacy, an uneasy divide that to some of us feels as porous and inconstant as a frayed tatter of gauze. The minions of chaos threaten to cross over at every turn, lurking in the cheating spouse, the undiscovered tumor, the murderous dictator, the brewing tornado, the salmonella in the Christmas turkey, the leak in the brake line. At any given moment, life is falling apart as fast as we're shoring it up.

"Self-mutilation may sometimes be a creative act linked with the restructuring of chaos into . . . order," writes Armando Favazza in his study of self-mutilation, *Bodies Under Siege*.

Not that any of these points necessarily brings us closer to an answer.

I can tell you that I am far from alone, that there are cutters and biters, pickers and pokers, bangers and breakers and burners and pullers and prickers. Some of us are specialists in our chosen method, and some of us care only to get the job done and will take whatever's handy. Have you ever wanted to punch the wall, pull your hair out? Don't think you might not be one of us.

I can tell you that the "typical" self-mutilator, the textbook case, is someone just like me: young, female, probably with an eating disorder thrown in (but that's another chapter), who started cutting sometime early in adolescence.

I can enumerate the various theories of self-mutilation, the sociocultural and the psychosexual, the biogenetic and the family-dynamic, all of them argued ardently by their various proponents armed with statistical charts and case studies.

Would any of these details really explain why?

I can offer you, as I have, my little penny-ante repertoire of teenage troubles. Collectively or individually, however, do they constitute sufficient grounds for taking up self-mutilation? Even as I set forth these explanations, I want to withdraw them again. I think what I thought when I was twelve, and thirteen, and fifteen, and twenty: None of these is reason enough, none of these is legitimate cause.

Well, how many troubles *should* equal a legitimate reason for self-mutilation? Ten? Twenty? One hundred? And how monumental must these troubles be? There's probably no critical mass beyond which cutting yourself would ever seem, to most people, like a reasonable choice. I cut because it did look that way to me. I cut because something had to give. I cut because the alternatives were worse.

We're always looking for the logical explanation, the smoking gun, the inscrutably sagacious detective who will reveal all in the final chapter—but some things are too complex to suffer reduction to a simple equation of why/because. I know that cutting was my defense against an internal chaos, against a sense of the world gone out of control. What I can't tell you is where that chaos came from, what exact balance of factors blew up the maelstrom of my mind. Maybe what drove me to cut doesn't have any cause I can name. Maybe it oozed up from nowhere, from within my blood, my cells, my very DNA.

Our family tree is hung with cranks and eccentrics, the merely batty, the existentially despondent, and so on down the precipitous decline to the drinkers and depressives and suicides. My father, in trying to explain to me once how I was related to a distant cousin, took me along a genealogical pathway strewn with bodies, including one entire family done in by razor and rope and revolver. So maybe I got my father's eyes, my mother's nose, and in the bargain an altogether murkier inheritance.

I suffered homesickness so extreme when I was a child that it bordered on panic, with frantic midnight calls begging my parents to come rescue me from wherever I had been invited to spend the night. I was paralyzingly afraid of the dark, and sometimes visited by nightmares so vivid and strangely disturbing that I can remember them still in almost perfect detail. I was so easily and thoroughly absorbed into the imagined world of my books or my toys that the lived world sometimes felt less real to me. It was an absolute policy of mine that I would not read any book in which the animal died in the end. In retrospect, should we have understood these things as indicators of a mind playing in the wrong key? Or is it only in retrospect that they start to look odd?

On a trip to West Virginia once, I stopped at the place billed as the official headwater of the Potomac—a paltry spurt of water burbling up into a trickle of a stream choked by winter leaves. In the end, if we could ever really pursue the question *why* to its true headwaters, we might find it is often no more than this: a beginning so trifling that it hardly bears notice. The flip of a switch. The flash of a neurotransmission. Maybe there was always something amiss, like a bulb planted and forgotten that blooms when the season is right. I can't stop wondering what, if anything, about who I've become was written inevitable into my chromosomes, lying in lurk, waiting for the apparently insignificant event that triggers an endless cascade of consequences. A thousand girls could have gotten through my seventh grade and breezed on with a laugh; I didn't. I sometimes think I carried my unhappiness with me like a portmanteau, and finally unpacked it in the heart of an unfortunate year.

12

Once I started cutting, I never considered that I might stop. I didn't want to stop. Why should I? Cutting was my deliverance, my knight-errant riding in on a bag of disposable Bics. I cut, and just like that the itching, anxious restlessness was gone. I cut, and was made paradoxically whole.

I cut, and then I could get up and get through the day and eat my dinner and complete my homework, because that's what you do. It was what was expected of me. It was what *I* expected of me. I could never have failed that duty, even when I wanted to. I would not have ventured the temerity to believe that my troubles justified a failure to meet my obligations. Those obligations drove me like a bus I couldn't get off; cutting was the fare that made it possible for me to stay on the bus I couldn't get off.

I cut often—maybe not every day, but every few days, or every week. You might imagine that a person would resort to self-mutilation only under extremes of duress, but once I'd crossed that line the first time, taken that fateful step off the precipice, then almost any reason was a good enough reason, almost any provocation was provocation enough. Cutting was my all-purpose solution.

My scars ought to be a charm bracelet of mnemonics, each a permanent reminder of its precipitating event, but maybe the most disturbing thing I can say about the history of my cutting is that for the most part I can't even remember the whens and the whys behind those wounds.

It didn't take much to make me cut. Frustration, humiliation, insecurity, guilt, remorse, loneliness—I cut 'em all out. They were like a poison, caustic and destructive, as though lye had been siphoned into my veins. The only way I could survive them, I thought, was to keep draining them from my blood.

I cut for a bad day in B^1—which was almost any day in B^1. I cut for the wrong answer on a test, for failing to be cast in the spring musical, for the way my nemeses among my schoolmates taunted me for that failure, cornering me in the parking lot after school and jeering, "Caroline didn't get ca-ast, Caroline didn't get ca-ast," in jubilant singsong. I cut for the humiliation of having given them the satisfaction of breaking down and sobbing in response.

I cut for the evening that the boarding-school boy I didn't even know settled insinuatingly next to me on the lobby sofa, while his friends clustered sniggering at the foot of the three wide, polished granite steps leading up to the lobby from the wide hallway below. I remember his loud plaid sports jacket, his smug self-satisfaction. He pulled out his wallet, extracted a ten-dollar bill. I remember wondering in that moment where he got a ten-dollar bill, when the weekly school allowance came in increments of four.

"Come to my room later," he said, proffering the bill, barely restraining his amusement at his own wit. He glanced to his friends for approval; their eyes shone with a hungry excitement at the daring of his innuendo.

It was such a cliché: the mannish insult to my woman's virtue. I felt a slow, sinking despair at the calculated spite that had gone into it. I didn't even know this boy, and yet he had gone out of his way to humiliate me here. What had I ever done to merit his cheap malice?

I cut for the day I overheard several girls at school, girls I had supposed were my friends, taking me apart piece by piece, itemizing my apparently abundant shortcomings with the delight of gourmands sampling exquisite delicacies.

"She thinks she's so special," one sneered.

"She's always writing in that stupid notebook."

"She's always talking about those stupid boys she knows."

"Don't you hate the way she's always showing off? It's like she *always* has to say something in class."

Unaware of my presence just around the corner, they picked gleefully over each and every one of my lengthily enumerated faults until they were left licking my figurative bones. I was mesmerized by the awfulness of it, the way you watch an accident unfold when you can do nothing to prevent it. So I cut as one slashes at snakebites, to drain the venom from my skin.

I cut when the Boys, my boys, put on their blue blazers for the last time that year, applauded the graduates, greeted their parents, stripped their beds, loaded up trunks and rooftop racks, and suddenly all were strangers to me, the world beyond our gates reasserting itself in families I'd never met, bored teenage sisters and gangly pubescent brothers and moms in luminescent green pants standing by directing while the dads wrestled luggage and stereos into the backs of station wagons. I stood forlornly at a distance, like a spy, knowing that I had no place in this piece of their lives. Then they drove off leaving too much emptiness, too much screaming silence, and I had to cut that out of me as well.

I cut when my parents announced that we would be moving off campus in the fall, to an apartment in Charlottesville. To my parents, it was just one more move. To me, it meant giving up my home. A bleak, unbearable vision threw itself up before me: some drab, institutional cinder-block cell of an apartment, like the military housing where we'd visited friends one summer, with broken-down plastic furniture and a forlorn square of yard scratched to bare dirt and hordes of grubby children with snotty noses. I cut for dread of the future.

You'd think that once you'd taken up self-mutilation, such an extreme gesture would color the rest of your life. Aside from the cutting, however, every other feature of my life was utterly, ordinary twelve. I had a big crush on John-Boy Walton. I did my homework. I got A's on all my report cards. I bought K-Tel records at the Woolco in Charlottesville. I went to slumber parties. I coveted a Radio Shack portable tape recorder and a pair of cork-soled platform shoes like the ones Susan Rhodes had worn to school last week. I read Dorothy Sayers murder mysteries, drank my milk, and wrote bad poetry.

I look at a photograph of me from that year, and I'm amazed by just how ordinary everything does look. There are all my animal posters plastered on my bedroom walls. The sun is pouring through the windows. My Flower Power curtains are just visible, and my clothes are thrown over my oak rocking chair, and just out of sight I know is the trash can my mother had given me as a joke with PLEASE, PLEASE PICK UP YOUR ROOM! printed on it in letters of ascending size and increasingly loud colors. It's a room that says "twelve-year-old girl" in every particular. Even the girl in the picture, with her hands on her hips, looks twelve, and as if she might just have been laughing with her father, who is taking the picture.

But there was this other Caroline who was tearing herself apart, who saw only the gray winter sky and the steady progression of her despondence. Why can't I remember our family Christmas, or a warm spring day, or anything that might have been pleasant? It is as though the filter of recall is itself altered, so that it blocks out everything but the darkest colors of the spectrum. My unhappiness precluded all else; unhappiness is a kind of narcissism, in which nothing that does not resonate with your unhappiness can interest you.

It's probably very hard to take a brooding twelve-year-old's miseries too seriously. The maudlin poetry. The dramatic excesses. The twelveness of it all.

It's just a stage, they'll tell you. *You'll get over it,* they'll tell you.

All that may be true, but the trouble is that at twelve you only know how to be unhappy in twelve-year-old ways—it doesn't make your unhappiness, to you, any less significant.

I scowled and moped and brooded, and I'm sure that my whole family found me a trial to live with, and I hated myself for this sullenness but I couldn't help it. I suffered a monstrous sense of grievance that every single thing existed for the express purpose of thwarting my happiness. This gnawing distress was so unlike anything I'd ever had to endure that I couldn't believe it really belonged to me, as though it were an ill-fitting suit of clothes wrongly delivered to my address.

So when I cut, each time I thought, *There, that'll do it,* certain I'd rid myself of this alien unhappiness for good. For a remarkably long time I continued to believe this, so that when the unhappiness came back, as it always did, it took me utterly by surprise.

I spent a lot of time lurking in my bedroom, festering with an anger that had no clear cause or object. I wrote long bewildered plaints in my journal, by the bilious green light cast by a souvenir lamp we'd bought at the beach one summer—meant to resemble a lighthouse lantern—with a bottle-green base illuminated by a night-light bulb. My old console stereo scratched out muddy refrains from the records I'd borrowed from one boy or another— *The White Album,* "Stairway to Heaven," the plaintive refrains of Bread singing "Everything I Own"—while I crouched on the floor by my bed, excising my troubles inch by inch, the blood beading black by the green light.

Sometimes one cut was enough, and in the wake of it I felt washed clean. Sometimes, however, I had to experiment to find just the right equation of placement and length and depth, and sometimes I simply needed more than one. Three or four dark threads in perfect parallel might transgress the plane of my skin. Some cuts were hardly more than scratches. Others pressed down through epidermis and dermis, down past the advance guard of surface capillaries, down into the thick of the subcutaneous domain.

Though sometimes I wanted to go deeper, I made certain my cuts were nothing I couldn't reasonably pass off, if necessary, as a bad cat scratch or an accidental brush with some sharp protrusion. I never cut so deep that I couldn't attend to the wounds myself: simple pressure to slow the bleeding, the injured body marshaling its arsenal of defenses, a complex chemistry to make, like the setting of wax upon a letter, first the easily broken gel of a clot and then the firm seal of the scab.

I cut only where I could hide the evidence under clothing: high on my arms and hips and legs. I had to keep my cutting secret; I knew I couldn't expect anyone else to understand. They'd want the reason I couldn't offer, the explanation I didn't have.

For some reason, I believed that I had above all else an obligation to protect everyone—my teachers, my family—from the knowledge of my cutting. What they did not know would not cause them pain.

14

It's easy for me now to offer up my explanations and analyses—
I've had almost a quarter of a century to think on it. When I started,
however, I had no idea, really, why I was cutting. I just knew it
was what I had to do.

I wasn't blind to the fact that it looked pretty crazy to be cutting
yourself like that, but it puzzled me that I didn't *feel* the least bit
crazy. You had to be pretty crazy, didn't you, to keep cutting
yourself with a razor blade?

Maybe, I thought, the cutting was just the first harbinger of
craziness, like the preliminary spatter of raindrops that presages a
sudden downpour. I kept testing gingerly around the edges of my
mind for evidence of craziness, as one might progress cautiously
across boggy ground. Any sign of a soft spot here, a spot likely to
give way?

If I wasn't crazy, then why was I doing something so obviously nutty? It bothered me that I couldn't ferret out my own motivations, as if they were being hidden from me the way a doctor won't let you see your own medical chart. I couldn't even decide for sure if I really did *need* to cut, or if I was just doing it to be dramatic.

As I sat hunched over my arm or my leg with the razor blade, I argued back and forth with myself as though I were the topic at hand in moot court.

You're just cutting to look crazy, I accused myself, as the blade bit through my skin.

Isn't cutting yourself inherently crazy, though? I asked in my defense. *How sane can you be if you're cutting yourself to prove you're crazy?*

That only proves your craftiness, the prosecution riposted. *You have to act crazy in crazy ways, after all, to look crazy.*

The way I saw it, the only way to prove the validity of my cutting was to keep it an absolute secret. If I told anyone, somehow let it slip, then right there in the telling would be the evidence that I was cutting only for the melodrama of it, cutting for attention— because once you admitted to these things, didn't the very act of admission render them suspect?

I knew, without being able to put the matter into so many words, that no one would believe me if I told them . . . what? That I kept a razor wrapped in a gauze pad, secreted away in a green steel file box, underneath a stack of three-by-five index cards I used as flash cards for Spanish I? That with the razor I kept little squares of blood-soaked gauze, dried to a rust-brown, like powerful relics? That sometimes, in the bathroom, I would cut myself, and standing in front of the mirror smear the blood in long, livid streaks across my face?

15

At the end of seventh grade I left my private school. It seemed ridiculous to pay good money to a private school to make you miserable. In the fall, I would transfer into a middle school in the Charlottesville public system—at least, in public school, the misery is free.

My sister had just finished ninth grade at Charlottesville High School; its spanking-new facilities, painted in relentlessly bright reds and yellows and greens, with exotic amenities like the Media Center and a television studio (which no one ever used, but that was beside the point), looked so much more modern and sophisticated than the tired cinder-block beiges of my private school.

In my seventh-grade class, however, was a girl who had transferred in from the city schools. Invested with the exotic, worldly-wise cachet of having come from those wild unknowns, she was like a war refugee, captivating us with horrific tales of public school life. She painted a picture of teeming, restless masses, of a school year punctuated by riots and cafeteria fights and the occasional knifing.

I was terrified of this new school, and yet eager to go. In the academic paradigm by which my life was regulated, the world began over again every September. There was a new schedule for your days, and people you hadn't seen in months came back taller or tanned, in new clothes, and people you'd never known before became a new part of your life. You had new books and pencils, new paper and notebooks, new shoes. Every September was a chance to remake yourself.

At this new school, no one knew me. For all they knew, I could be the aloof, cool, even mysterious me that I planned to be. I imagined myself wearing a wistful, knowing smile when people spoke to me, a smile that hinted at desperate tragedies painfully mastered. I even practiced the smile in the mirror. I wouldn't be unfriendly, just subtly detached, removed, as though I had seen far, far too much of the world for eighth grade to be more than a mere precious amusement. My fellow eighth-graders would cast sidelong glances at me, intrigued by this quiet figure moving with subdued dignity through each day.

She was nothing more than another invented, third-person Caroline, conjured up with the idea that she could somehow resolve the inconsistency between my emotional state and my pedestrian, middle-schooler's life. As if it couldn't be possible to be a tortured soul with your rubber bands forever snapping off your braces. As if, in order to validate your unhappiness, you had to be a dedicated postulant to misery alone, with no extracurricular distractions.

———

After the feverish intensity of the preceding months, summer fell across my lap like a corpse. I'd always loved summers in the past, the endless indolent hours stretching before me in languid promise. The ratcheting whir of cicadas filled the air, and the cement of the porch was cool under my feet as I pushed myself in lazy arcs on the hammock, absorbed in an Agatha Christie.

Now my misery robbed me of even this pleasure, and summer offered the prospect of nothing but endless empty hours made worse because instead of spending the season, as we always had, in Virginia, we were heading for Saratoga Springs in upstate New York, where my father's relatives lived. I'm sure there must have been discussions leading up to this event; my parents had bought a small house there, divided into rental apartments. One of these was to be made available to students during the school year and reserved for us in the summer. In my memory, however, the whole proposal drops on me like a leaden fait accompli.

I suspect that if we had stayed home I would still have spent the summer in a dismal state. Nevertheless, I saw Saratoga as the latest outrage against me. I found its town-ness unnerving, with all those cars and all those strangers and the world gridded into streets and sidewalks and little green squares of front lawns. It felt at once both too restrictive and too full of unknowns—anything might happen to you, and the worst thing was that you couldn't even know what the dangers were and so couldn't know what to do to avoid them.

But no matter. I wasn't planning on going anywhere or doing anything. I was going to spend the whole summer drooped like a wilted stalk of celery across the frameless mattress that was my bed, staring hatefully at the blank white wall and playing Bread's "Baby I'm-a Want You" endlessly on my prized secondhand stereo that I'd bought from my cousin. That was my plan, and to leaven my days I'd brought along my trusted, stamped-steel companion. To disinfect the blade, I dabbed it with a cotton ball dipped in Love's Lemon Scent, so that the faint sting of alcohol and a cool lemony essence served as markers to each cutting interlude. I was cutting the way kids will hang around smoking—to pass the time, to fill the empty hours.

My plan was to wallow in boredom, to wear my boredom like a hair shirt, to explore every flat plane and dull shade of boredom. In spite of my dedicated plans, however, I found myself in short order palling around with some of the kids on the block. I was intrigued by the small-town novelty of it all: ambling down to the Rexall for sodas, to the state fair across town, to the movies and the mall. *Here I am,* said my Narrator, *hanging out with the Gang.*

I went to my first concert, that teenage rite of passage—America, opened by Captain & Tennille—with my new friend Lewis, and afterward as we were sitting in my backyard talking about not much in particular he leaned over suddenly and tried to kiss me.

I spun away as though bitten, my reaction as startling to me as to him. Why did I feel a flash of panic? He stammered some kind of apology. I stammered some kind of excuse.

Was that kiss the catalyst, the very last straw?

One July day thereafter, hot and airless in our first-floor apartment, I sat on the living room sofa with a plate propped on my lap, eating a ham sandwich. Thick slab of smoky-sweet pink ham, crisp iceberg lettuce, smeared with a gelatinous glob of mayonnaise and poised in the embrace of two thick hunks of homemade bread. I can assure you there was never a sandwich more multifaceted in its charms, more seductive in its flavors, than this, the last sandwich of my lost gustatory innocence.

I licked a few, final mayonnaise-y crumbs from my fingers with great satisfaction, and then it occurred to me:

You're fat.

As though a distorted fun-house mirror had just been thrown up in front of me, I saw with sudden and perfect clarity the image of my self: grotesque, bloated, the embodiment of ill-restraint. As if the whole last year had been winding up to this moment of confrontation, as if I'd been fleeing headlong from a horror, then turned the corner to find I had been running all this time from my own self.

Time and space blurred, suspended. I lay on the sofa in almost a fugue state, thinking, *I will stop eating. I will stop eating.* I wasn't trying to convince myself; it was a statement of fact. I did not say to myself that I would go on a diet. I did not say that I would lose weight. Simply, I would not eat. This decision seemed so perfectly obvious that it was like suddenly coming up with the Grand Unified Theory. Of course! How could I not have understood this before?

I weighed ninety-eight pounds, which at five feet two inches would have been stretching the definition of fat. Nevertheless, it was fat to me, so I would stop eating until I weighed seventy-five. Seventy-five was the number I settled on from that first moment. It was the number I associated with that other, lost life, the one I had lived on the previous side of twelve.

Imagine if you could truly make yourself indifferent to want. It is desire, say the Buddhists, that makes us suffer. I want, I need, I hunger—I suffer. Imagine how ridding yourself of desire would ease the burden of living. So I chose to believe—I had to believe, it was the number I would place all my chips on—that I could eradicate hunger, that it was something utterly distinct from self, something I could jettison like so much unneeded ballast. I knew it was possible. I knew it was necessary. Thinness would be the visible mark of my self-perfection. All I had to do was strip myself down to the simple mathematics of line and angle, the essential, the prime number of self.

I stopped just like that. The next morning I woke up, and I didn't eat. Every morning after that I woke up and didn't eat. It was startlingly easy. It gave me something interesting to occupy the rest of the summer. I spent all of every day working on not eating.

I did allow for certain minor exceptions to the general rule of refusal: diet root beer, a smallish tangerine, one carefully measured cup of plain yogurt. All that other food, it was dangerous. When I fell to its temptation, when I succumbed to a scoop of curried eggs over rice or a creamy wedge of sharp New York cheddar, it was as though I had wallowed in some corrupt orgy of appetite.

By the logic of my obsession, however, food consumed without witnesses did not exist. At the dinner table I'd push three bites listlessly around my plate; then later, alone in the kitchen lit dimly by the open refrigerator door, I'd frantically stuff handfuls of that same food into my mouth, poised like a scavenger to flee at the sound of approaching footsteps. Technically, of course, I was witness to this eating, but somehow it seemed entirely possible to deceive even myself.

Emptiness was what I sought. Emptiness, like a pure note plucked from a perfectly strung instrument. I lay on my bed for hours at a time, experiencing emptiness. My days were occupied with delaying as long as possible the moment when I would finally rise in my emptiness to walk to the kitchen, my feet whispering like air along the wood floors, to withdraw that one, cold carton of yogurt from the refrigerator and spoon it up in excruciatingly slow bites, letting each one dissolve away on my tongue before finally I swallowed.

The narrowness of my obsession was a part of its appeal: I would be about nothing but refusal. To hold hunger in abeyance felt like a power of incomparable magnitude. I will, therefore I am.

In the endless idle hours of August I imagined over and over again how I would walk into that first day of my new school. I'd never even seen the place, so I sketched in vague details to stand for the buildings and the furniture and the teachers. All these details were irrelevant, anyway. The point of the portrait, its very center, drawn in every shadow and detail, was my slenderness. I liked those sibilant thin words. *Slender. Slim. Slight.*

16

Public school turned out to be—well, school. It was louder and bigger and more institutionally characterless than my old school, and packs of tough girls cruised the hallways, lumpish in too-tight jeans, with lank Farrah Fawcett haircuts, long-handled combs stuck in their rear pockets. But when you get right down to it, English Grammar and Comp is pretty much English Grammar and Comp wherever you find it.

My father brought me on the first day. The two of us sat in the front office waiting for my class schedule, while I watched tides of middle-schoolers sweeping past the office door in a cacophony of shouts and a whiff of grape bubble gum. It was all so very . . . *public.* The great, undifferentiated masses.

My heart froze at the prospect of being tossed into that tide. I wanted to beg my father to take me with him, not to abandon me here, but to return me to the hateful familiarity of my old school and my former tormentors. Instead, I waited politely, and then a student aide slouched up to show me to my homeroom, and my father gave me a kiss and a smile of encouragement and I was swallowed up in that sea.

Tears stung my eyes as I followed the aide through a labyrinth of hallways. How would I ever know where anything was? I felt so abjectly alone, as though I had been transported to a foreign land, lost forever to friends and family.

That lasted about three days, during which time I completely abandoned any pretense at cool, aloof, wistful knowingness in an effort simply to make it through the day without bursting into tears, and then I was taken under the wing of a cheerful girl named Mary who shared my homeroom, a girl with a bright and bustling manner and thickly curled hair and a mission to be my guide through the perils of public school. She told me whom to ignore and whom to avoid, which bathrooms were safest, which teachers were coolest, and most kindly of all, and to my eternal gratitude, insisted that I join her and her friends at their lunch table. There are few things more desolate, more forlorn, than sitting alone in a school lunchroom.

These girls became my friends, truly the nicest girls in the eighth grade, the most decent and generous and cheerful girls. I selectively edited all that I believed was sordid and bitter and caustic in me— the scarlet past, the suicidal dreams, the razor, the self-starvation— so that I could take shelter in their warmth and good spirits. In their company, I could script myself, could almost even imagine myself, as just another bookish eighth-grader, with no more momentous preoccupation than the next day's algebra quiz.

My best friend among these girls was English by birth, and I loved the Briticisms that inflected her speech, the way she said "alumin-i-um" with the extra "i" and "herbs" with the "h" pronounced. She was smart, and she had a wonderful bedroom tucked into the eaves of her family's house, with window seats in the dormers that begged for curling up with a good book. There wasn't anything mawkishly girlish about her, just that wonderful, sturdy

British good sense and competence, like a pair of stout and reliable brogues, to guide her. I felt chronically grateful to be her friend. Everything about her from her mastery of mathematics to her neatly ordered brown-bag lunches spoke of a level head and a reasonable relationship with the world.

Never once in the years that we were friends would I have thought even for a moment to tell her of that other life of mine, the one that unfolded by the light of my lighthouse lamp and the measure of my scales. That life might almost not have existed, except for its secret reminders to me etched out in scab and scar tissue and the ever-present racket in my head.

Every now and then, one of these Very Nice Girls would remark on my shrinking body and my miserly lunches.

"You're so skinny," Mary would say, as I hunched over my cup of yogurt or my tiny jewel of tangerine, "you need to eat something. Here, take part of my sandwich."

I wanted that sandwich, I wanted the slabs of hamburger-topped pizza and the thick cheeseburgers and the french fries limp with grease that came off the cafeteria line. But I'd wave them away, and I'd wave away the sandwich or the cookies or the chips Mary was always trying to offer.

"Oh, God, no thanks. I had such a *huge* breakfast, you wouldn't believe. I'm still so full I can't even finish this tangerine." And I'd push away the last little crescent moon of fruit, with a secret surge of delighted triumph.

My project for Mr. Wayne's general science class was my diet. We were assigned to measure and record the progress of something—anything—over the course of the school year. I would measure the progressive and eagerly anticipated disappearance of my body.

"MY DIET," I printed in large, commanding block letters across the cover of an electric-blue spiral notebook. That's what I called it, that's what I believed it—a diet. Inside the notebook, under each day and date, I listed "Breakfast," "Lunch," "Dinner," and then the shameful evidence of my still-unmastered appetites: one apple—100 calories; two olives—16 calories; one saltine—12 calories. I carried everywhere a little pocket calorie guide, which I consulted until I had it memorized, panicking when something I ate was not listed, thinking that if I wasn't absolutely certain of the precise number of calories I consumed, then anything could happen. Anything.

In the right-hand column I entered my weight, and each day as I sat with my pen poised, ready to inscribe the number, I struggled between scrupulous, merciless honesty and generous optimism. I weighed myself every morning, stark naked, e-e-easing onto the scale as though I might surprise it into dropping five pounds off me, just like that. If the needle hovered just a fraction of an inch above the black line that represented 91 pounds, could I go ahead and put myself down as 91? Or was that cheating? How could I wrap myself in the brief glory of 91, when clearly I still clung to the last bloated vestiges of 92? You cannot imagine how much time I gave to such debates.

I looked in the mirror every day, poking and prodding at my too-abundant flesh, searching for the emerging protrusion of bone. I looked in the mirror and the girl who looked back seemed familiar, yes, but not overly familiar. Certainly not intimately familiar. Not at all what I knew myself to be.

——————

If you want to call it anorexia, you'd probably be safe enough. An eating disorder, let's say, to be accurate without overstating the case.

I'd never heard of such a thing as an eating disorder then, and even if I had, I doubt I would have connected the term in any way to my own behavior. I'm sure I would have assumed I didn't qualify. I lost nearly twenty pounds in five months, but what's that? Four pounds a month, one pound a week, big deal. I never made it below eighty pounds. I never ended up in a hospital, jammed full of tubes, pitting my will against reward systems and group therapy.

I don't care to claim that I had anorexia, because I worry that I'll be challenged on the point and discounted on a technicality. After I first read about it, in *Seventeen* magazine a few years later, I would recite the diagnostic criteria to myself like so many Stations of the Cross, suspecting all along that true anorexia was not for the likes of me, that it was reserved for those more troubled than I, whose suffering was greater.

Did my parents see what I was doing? Did I eat more, or less, than I believed? Did I hide myself well, or make myself obvious? I remember my father sometimes harping on me to eat, but the more I was urged to eat, the more triumphant I felt in refusing. Having something to push off against made me stronger.

During that school year my family was dividing our life between an apartment in Charlottesville and our campus home. I'd wake up in the morning, and my mother would already be rushing out the door to make her classes twenty-five miles away, my father long since gone. It was easy to skip breakfast, or to dawdle in the apparent act of toasting an English muffin, and then stuff it, barely nibbled, wrapped in a paper towel to disguise it, into the bottom of the trash can. My sister, whose metabolism could have burned through a steel door, churned up thick breakfast shakes of whole milk and eggs and chocolate sauce and instant coffee, and sat at the table sipping her meal, elaborately ignoring me.

Lunch was an easy lie; I told my friends I'd eaten at home and I told my parents I'd eaten at school if it ever occurred to them to ask. Dinner was more problematic. I didn't want to have to look at food, to find myself in too-dangerous proximity to it, and I was thankful for all the many days when dinner was a haphazard scrounging affair shoehorned in between my parents' academic schedules and my sister's extracurriculars.

I could lie about my eating with perfect equanimity, my gaze level as I improvised my prevarications. "I had a big snack when I got home from school. I'll make myself something later."

Once you take to the habit of deception, every new lie comes that much easier. Though to me it wasn't so much lies as a matter of judicious editing. We all inevitably present a version of ourselves that is a collection of half-truths and exclusions. The way I saw it, the truth was too complicated, whereas the well-chosen lie would put everyone's mind at ease. Why gum up the works with information nobody wants?

17

Anorexia isn't about *being* fat, it's about *having* fat. Any fat. Any bulge or fold or wrinkle that isn't skin, muscle, or bone. Fat's too dangerous. It's too amorphous. It has no structure, it dimples and jiggles and droops. It is born of a disturbing, invisible alchemy, by which a cracker, a slice of cake, a pickle, a ham sandwich, all of it is rendered into the same tallow congealed beneath your skin. Fat gets away from you. You could almost imagine that it replicates itself, that once you lay down that first layer, your fat will take over from there. You could imagine yourself consumed by it, swallowed and suffocated by it, pulled down and drowned in it. Fat does not negotiate, it rampages.

Therefore the only way to be sure you are safe from it is to allow none of it, not one ounce or curve of it. You must strip yourself to skin stretched like a canvas on a frame of bone, and even then you have fought merely to a stalemate, a permanent demilitarized zone along which you must stand vigilant at all times. You have to stake out your border.

My eating disorder was driven by a blind, animal need like the one that fueled my cutting—something far below the level of conscious thought that hounded me day and night with a desperate urgency, an alarm going out. It was vital not to eat; I understood that one fact with pristine clarity. It wasn't a point that required further clarification; it was, as I saw it, my life's one Truth.

Anorexia is not about being pretty. It's not about being desirable. It's not even about being thin, really, because "thin" doesn't begin to describe what you're aiming for. Thin is too transient, too untrustworthy, too liable to slip away from you in a bite here, a nibble there. What you want is bone: absolute, impermeable, the Maginot line. Anorexia is not for the weak.

I learned, just a few years ago, that among self-mutilators, as many as sixty percent report a parallel history of eating disorders: a statistic that didn't surprise me. From the outside, their shared theme might appear to be self-destruction, but from where I've stood, what they have in common is something altogether different. I subdued hunger, overcame the animal self's blind instinct for self-preservation, in search of a perfect silence.

18

Our apartment in Charlottesville took up half of a nondescript, ranch-style brick duplex in a small, characterless neighborhood hemmed in by commercial strips, professional offices, and an apartment complex. The kind of neighborhood occupied by recently divorced single mothers, and struggling young couples, and low-level-management bachelors edging into their forties and eating half-frozen TV dinners over the sink. And us, of course.

Our apartment had two dark bedrooms, a cramped bathroom, and a living-dining room opening into a kitchen. Electric-blue industrial-grade carpeting glued to the living room floor suggested the transience of so many tenant feet coming and going, short-timers too briefly in residence to care for comfort. The walls were covered in a paint textured with vicious little nubbins.

The worst thing about our apartment, however, was the suffocating feeling of confinement, of being reduced to a cramped space and a scrubby backyard imprisoned by chain-link fencing. It made me restless and claustrophobic. It was depressing. It wasn't home.

It was, on the other hand, an adventure. I lived in an *apartment*—so sophisticatedly urban. I didn't know anyone who lived in an apartment. I imagined we might have wacky neighbors and comic sitcom adventures in the manner of Mary Tyler Moore and her spun-off former neighbor, Rhoda. I could ride a bus to school, a proposition so Middle American that it sounded positively exotic. My sister and I could walk—walk!—to the Safeway just up the road. In the midst of my self-imposed starvation a grocery store was like pornography: so desirable, so forbidden.

We left virtually all our furniture out at our other house, which we continued to think of for a while yet as our *real* house, and my parents hammered together the trappings of domesticity in square-edged lumber: a sofa, and platform beds of particleboard resting on square two-by-four frames, topped with foam pads. I liked the novelty of sleeping only inches off the floor. I thought it was hip and chic and unconventional, very hippie vans and Haight-Ashbury. We even slept under sleeping bags.

That our parents had moved us to Charlottesville with the primary intention of wresting my sister and me from the oppressive attention of too many bored teenage boys was never discussed. That was the subject that dared not breathe its uncomfortable name—a La Brea Tar Pit of awkwardness all of us preferred not to blunder into.

"But *why* are we moving to Charlottesville?" I'd demanded, attempting to exploit this avoidance of the obvious answer to my advantage. As though if my parents couldn't come up with a good enough explanation, the whole plan might be scrapped. Why do children ever bother to mount such negotiations?

"You'll be close to school," said my mother. "You can be in plays, and your sister can play on the soccer team."

It was irritatingly difficult to argue against that logic. The long drive to Charlottesville had always been the bane of our extracurricular lives, the reason why we couldn't join Brownie troops or even attend birthday parties without planning as if for a military campaign.

Nevertheless, I burned with ill-concealed resentment at this move, which I considered to have been dreamed up if not quite for the sole purpose of making me unhappy, then at least in complete disregard of my feelings. I'd waited the whole summer in maddened impatience to get back to Virginia—back, plain and simple, to the boys. Life had gotten stupefyingly boring the minute they left school in the spring. I wrote some of them ten- and fifteen-page letters, the romantic inaccuracies of my memory of them growing exponentially with each further day of our separation. I crafted endless reunion fantasies for their return in the fall.

In the end, when I saw them again for the first time, we just stood around awkwardly, hands jammed in our pockets, trading labored barbs as though our repartee had grown rusty with disuse. Before long, however, we'd slipped comfortably back into familiar grooves. What surprises me is that none of them, after a summer's reflection and no doubt a fair crop of girls their own age, had grown too self-conscious to continue chatting up an eighth-grader with newly installed braces on her teeth. I had worried that those braces, along with the glasses I could no longer shirk wearing because I couldn't see the blackboard anymore even when I squinted, would spell my social death, but no, it was my parents who were ruining my life, with their relocation agenda.

———

In spite of our new apartment, we maintained technical occupancy of our house, and at first I seized any opportunity, any excuse to finagle a night or a weekend there.

"I need to go out to the house tonight to look for a book," I'd say, or "Wouldn't it be fun to go for a hike this weekend?" I'm not saying these pretexts weren't patently transparent, but at the time I believed they would appear credible.

Once on campus, I'd wait, my heart pounding with anticipation, for dinner, for walking into the dining room and imagining a little ripple, an awareness among my putative pals that I'd reappeared, as if they were dogs suddenly getting wind of something intriguing, and sniffing at the air. But of course you never look. Never acknowledge. Just feel like you are moving through an electrically charged field, its faint crackle and surge playing across your skin. Eat nothing, just sip slowly at your milk, because eating is so degrading, so empty of dignity.

After dinner, I'd meander to the lobby, maintaining the same requisite pretense of nonchalance. We'd warm up with a few moments of fidgety mock hostilities.

"Gee! We thought you were dead," they'd say, or "Oho! So you condescended to come back and see us!"

"Yeah, well, I'm stuck here for the weekend. Figured I had to kill time somehow," I'd say in reply.

The preliminaries dispensed with, we'd settle back into the same old routines, the thrusts and parries of our game.

But I'd reached fickle thirteen; my allegiances began to drift. Every time we stayed in our old home for the night or the weekend, the house seemed that much colder, emptier, more depressing. It took on a ghostly quality, like a house abandoned suddenly in the face of some oncoming cataclysm or lethal plague. One glass stood on the drainboard in the kitchen, rinsed and reused, rinsed and reused. The soap dried and cracked in the dish in the bathroom my sister and I had shared. My father, who stayed there the most, did his living in his bedroom and study, and the rest of the house went unheated. My room—still with its familiar array of animal posters on the wall, my childhood bed and desk, a few outgrown dresses hanging in the closet, the Trixie Belden novels stacked thick along the bookshelf, the Fisher-Price toys piled in the closet—seemed like an artifact preserved, a museum reconstruction of a life that was almost but not quite familiar, a life I could see but never revisit. An almost palpable pall of disuse settled like dust over everything. I think we even draped some of the furniture in sheets, though that may be my imagination.

When we first moved into the apartment, we brought with us the bare minimum of possessions, thinking in a vague way that, at some undetermined point in the future, when some unspecified criteria had been met, we would go home and resume our interrupted lives, like returning relieved from a disastrous vacation. Degree by degree, however, that life receded unrecoverable into our past. Each new possession we moved into our apartment signaled the shifting of worlds, until the balance had tipped unalterably.

Charlottesville was seductive in its charms. We could run up to the store for a quart of milk. I could walk to my best friend's house after school. Going to a movie? It's as easy as pie—just get your mother to drop you off into your little cluster of girlfriends all waiting there in line with ticket money and giggling gossip.

Then there were my sister's friends, a pack of flamboyant, brainy students from Charlottesville High School, who milled about one another in a constant ebb and flow of emotional drama. They fascinated me, with their complex theoretical ontologies and conversations that rambled broad and deep. The narrowly focused talk of the boarding-school boys started looking vapid and dull by comparison; it was only ever about sex and how much beer they would drink at their next vacation, and sex and the cars they would buy in college, and sex and the apartments they would inhabit then, and sex and the girls they would sleep with. And sex.

My sister's friends never talked about sex, except in wry, sophisticated double entendres. They chattered in French and argued vehemently about people I'd never heard of, with names like Voltaire and Nietzsche.

They were also entirely unlike *my* school friends, those level-headed girls whose intelligence never seemed to unsettle them from the calm procession of school and music lessons and two hours of studying after dinner. Those girls were my daytime friends, straightforward like the bright, defining light of day.

My sister's friends, however—into whose company I managed, somehow, gradually to insinuate myself, though I would always, nevertheless, think of them as "my sister's friends"—were night people. I can hardly remember a time that we were together when the sun was out. We'd drive around Charlottesville, all piled into the beat-up four-door owned by the one boy in the group who had both a license and a car. Then we'd spill out onto the night-shadowed grounds of the University of Virginia, or run around abandoned downtown streets. I remember running through the darkness and the occasional flash of light, breathless with excitement and the cold air raw in my throat. The rest of the city slept around us, oblivious, I thought, but we were alive to the nuanced nighttime subtleties of light and dark. I had stumbled across that startling power of being, simply, young, with all of life's possibilities still undecided and waiting.

I suppose we must have had curfews, but in my memory we stayed up half the night. My sister and I often slept over at our friend Madeleine's house; her parents apparently made no issue of our comings and goings. Her parents were, in fact, invisible as far as I can remember, their presence made known only through the endless supply of snack foods stocked in their vast kitchen, snacks I spent a great deal of time thinking about not eating.

During the day my sister's friends seemed more ordinary and even a bit odd, but at night they intrigued me as mysterious, troubled, brilliant, talking their rarified philosophies and carrying on in angst-saturated crises. My sister in particular had angst, buckets of angst, and she and one or another of her friends would come to some life-altering moment of confrontation standing under the cold light of a city streetlamp on an empty street with their voices echoing against darkened buildings.

Hunched on the hood of a car in the pale blue puff of my down jacket, I could never even begin to understand what the crises were about, but I could see that clearly they were very Deep and Meaningful and Important. Secretly, I kept worrying that I was always going to be just too ordinary for anything but my ordinary and second-best angst, and would live forever vicariously on the edges of things, in uneasy company with a bag of Cheez Doodles.

19

Having so long coveted it, now I couldn't imagine what I'd ever thought was so special about thirteen. Sure, we were the top of the heap at school, but that meant we were the top of nothing. *Middle* school: doesn't the name say it all? Now I could see that high school was where life truly began, and eighth grade was just another year of waiting to get older.

That being said, eighth grade, in spite of its girl gangs and chronic chaos and self-imposed starvation, was a good year. In the shelter of my little coterie of Very Nice Friends, I could see that a pleasantly normal world existed in which girls lived in their own homes and brought brown-bag lunches to school and had piano lessons before supper. I couldn't imagine that I would ever live that kind of life, nor did I exactly want to; I continued to believe that my family's persistent divergence from the norm was what made us interesting, as though not belonging were our essential defining feature. But I found proximity to that other life comforting. I could visit it, in the homes of my friends who did not sleep on homemade particleboard beds.

In the middle of eighth grade, I and several of my Very Nice Friends were tapped for a new enrichment program for gifted students, a class called Quest that met daily in a tiny glass cubicle off the library. Only some fifteen or so students in the entire middle school were offered a place in this class, and I'm happy to admit that my ego was exceedingly gratified by this singling out. I considered it one in the eye for my former grade school and the slow-learning debacle.

I can't remember much of what we did to enrich ourselves in Quest, except bask in the warm light of devoted, individualized attention from our teacher and her assistant. We did spend a lot of time writing, which allowed me ample opportunity to produce a copious body of morbid free verse. A lot of dark colors and bare branches and cold rain and colder hearts.

"Can't you write something more *cheerful?*" asked the assistant, a blond young thing who was probably doing her student-teaching rotation and was still brimful with optimism and idealism about shaping young minds.

In a Swiftian spirit, I slapped down a couple of verses about smooth yellow sunshine pouring like lemon butter across idyllic spring meadows. "Yummy!" I wrote on the final line with a flourish.

"Oh yes, that's so much nicer," she said delightedly.

I was very amused at myself.

At the end of the spring, Quest compiled a selection of our short stories into a mimeographed booklet to treasure always. After twenty-two years I do still have mine, slightly stained and worn, one painful piece of evidence from my eighth-grade self.

Set upon
> *by life's*
>> *joys,*

sorrows,

and perfections,

that find

their way

to paper

I wrote rather incomprehensibly at the front, and *To Caroline, Don't let anything get you down. I'm behind you 100%! CK,* I wrote more optimistically at the back. I signed my name and initials all over the book, part of an endless series of signings and practicings of my signature. I continued working at my signature for years, as though when I settled upon a signature I would settle upon a self.

The Quest oeuvre was, with the exception of one or two light-hearted entries, an alarming litany of the preoccupations of our middle-school minds. In one, a happy family's life is destroyed when the Communists take over. In another, a man digs up his dead wife, convinced she has been buried alive. In a third, a girl is stabbed to death with a butcher knife, the victim of a terrible family curse. In yet another, a boy's best friend is hit by a car and dies in a hospital-room denouement. One more story, a pithy one-pager, has a girl slash herself up with a razor blade so that the twelve other girls in her witch's coven can drink her blood until she's dead. And that wasn't even my story. In mine, an unhappy teenage girl with a mean sister and parents who just don't understand kills herself with a bottle of pills:

. . . the last rays of sunlight shone through Janet's bedroom window, illuminating the still body lying among the shattered glass and debris upon the floor.

"The Best of Quest," our little mimeographed masterpiece was called, and it wouldn't surprise me if our lead teacher went home and had a stiff drink after she'd read through it all. She took me aside one day at the end of class and asked me if there was anything, in light of my story, that I felt I would like to talk about. My story, she said, was very . . . vivid.

I liked my teacher. She was young, an exotic blend of ethnicities before such things were so common. But I wasn't falling for that "anything you want to talk about" line; down that road lay trouble and all kinds of explaining and self-extricating.

"It's just a story," I reassured her.

I even jokingly repeated the whole conversation to my parents that night, pointing out the hilarity of her suggestion to throw them off the scent in case they read my story.

Now, of course you could argue that simply by writing that story I'd shown my hand already, and that if I truly wanted to keep my troubles to myself, I would have churned out something more along the lines of the "Yummy!" poem. But at the time my favorite reading was all suicides and madness: *Lisa, Bright and Dark*; *I Never Promised You a Rose Garden*. I figured if a story didn't end with someone dead or crazy, how good could it be? An opinion apparently shared by most of the rest of Quest. What is it about insanity and untimely death that so captures the imagination of young girls?

———————

I do believe there are people for whom misery is a calling, who are born to it, who make it a life's work, relishing the entire spectrum of woe. I, on the other hand, wore my troubles uneasily, almost couldn't quite believe in them. They troubled me plenty, certainly, but I always felt vaguely bewildered and beleaguered by them, as though I'd woken up one morning and found myself saddled with someone else's miserable life. Surely this unhappiness was meant for someone . . . well, for someone more characteristically suited for the job? Surely I was not apt enough an apprentice, always trying to shirk my solemn duties with an irreverent gibe at my own expense?

I suppose, then, that what I aspired to, in my romantic and literary notions of madness, was something more poetic and somehow explicable than this grinding discontent I'd been stuck with.

I kept my cutting so resolutely to myself not because I feared *its* discovery, per se, but rather because I knew it would be like the fatally ill-timed sneeze that gives the heroine away when she most needs to escape detection. It would be the signpost to a whole inner life I could neither justify nor explain, a life that was like one of those "find the item that doesn't match" games.

I credit chronic despair for my sense of humor; the more my preoccupations consumed me, the more I endeavored to suggest the opposite, to appear blithe and irreverent, to strike up a jaunty tune even while the ship went down. I mounted a public self whose job it was to distract attention from any evidence of that other me. I'm not saying I mastered elusiveness all in one stroke; instead, I assembled it piece by piece. I learned to smooth over the gaps, to skim the surface. It's the storyteller's art to present a coherent narrative, to omit the details that divert from the chosen trajectory.

I set about making myself a one-girl masquerade, quipping and capering, jesting and gibing, dancing merrily from one topic to the next and never alighting for long on any one thing. Indeed, anytime gravity threatened at all, I would fling a wry quip into the breach like a flare shot up to explode the darkness.

I did send-ups of my teachers, of the chaos of life at Walker, of the mountainous teacher's aide who drifted off to sleep every day during algebra, of the poor, mooning, lovesick boy in my class who called me every night with nothing to say, but could not hang up. I was nice enough that I couldn't tell him not to bother, but not so nice that I didn't make antic faces at my family and roll my eyes as the empty conversation dragged on.

Humor is a high-energy pursuit, an on-your-toes kind of calling, one step ahead of the repo man. Slice off a deftly timed one-liner and everybody's laughing. How gratifying it is to amuse. How easy it gets to toss off a witticism to ease any awkwardness, to sidestep any solemnity. When you amuse, it even seems, for the briefest possible moment, that you are who you appear to be, so clever and confident and at ease. No one ever asks difficult questions or takes you to task or enumerates your shortcomings while laughing. People like to be amused. They *prefer* to be amused. You can avoid whole categories of the anxiety-inducing by keeping the laughs coming like an endless round of champagne on the house. Then while your court jester of a self is mumming out front, the rest of you can slip out the stage door where you can't be found.

My family knew me as a certain, particular Caroline, and my friends and teachers knew me as slightly different but basically similar Carolines—flippant, generally reliable, maybe a bit moody around the house, but essentially unremarkable. Can I say that the apparent Caroline was any less authentic because certain details had been edited out? We all have a public face that varies to a greater or lesser degree from the one we show only to ourselves. How wide a divergence between the public and private must there be before we are guilty of living a lie?

Suppose you discovered that your husband, your wife, someone you love deeply, had once committed a terrible, an unforgivable crime. Yesterday, when you didn't know, you loved that person with all your heart. Today, you know. Nothing about the person you love has changed—all that has changed is what you know. One piece of information omitted can make all the difference in the world.

20

I could see that my life was looking up in every regard, with my Very Nice Friends, my academic successes, the delightful novelty of sheer, placid normalcy in the details of everyday life not lived in a boarding school, the steadily declining numbers on the bathroom scale. So why couldn't I escape this brooding, suffocating, featureless anxiety? If the origins of my unhappiness had been grounded in the tangible events of seventh grade, now that unhappiness had won a self-perpetuating life of its own. It was as though a groove had been worn into my mind, a path of least resistance down which I tumbled over and again, retracing the same wrong turns and dark corridors.

It was like being isolated in a very small and very bare room with someone extremely anxious, restless, and eager to find fault with me, who would pace and gesticulate and mutter a tireless

litany of recriminations and worries. The diatribe carried on un-
relenting day and night, flaring and dying away as if in an endless
Doppler effect. At its worst I would feel as if an entire chorus had
crowded into that cramped space with me to shriek and babble and
mill about wringing their hands at me, one among them chosen to
get up in my face and wail ceaselessly *What are you going to do what
are you going to do whatareyougoingtodo?!!*

Once, I saw a nature film in which wildebeest were driven mad
by a cloud of biting insects and ran bucking and flailing across the
plains until they dropped. That's the way this anxiety felt: unre-
lenting, like the swarming and torment of a thousand invisible mos-
quitoes, and it made me, too, want to run screaming and flailing
my arms. But I was not meant to be a screamer or a flailer—that
was too dramatic, way out of my league.

Sometimes, though, when the apartment was empty, I would
go into the bathroom and turn on all the faucets. Water rushed
into the sink, splashed into the tub, rattled and rained against the
curtain when I flipped the shower on. Amid this cascade, I stood
in front of the towel rack under the window, pressing a bright
yellow bath towel to my face, screaming and screaming into its
thick, muffling folds.

My sister and I shared a small bedroom in this apartment, a dark
space with one window facing the tired indirection of western light.
Accustomed to separate bedrooms, we chafed at each other in this
too-confined space. I lay on the cold wood floor at night, counting
my way through my daily one hundred sit-ups, dreaming of the
lost bedroom of my youth.

In this apartment, I cut with the jumpy alertness of a cat burglar,
ready to yank down a sleeve, palm a razor at the sound of approaching footsteps. In this apartment, I learned the expedience of
the quick and dirty cut job, the flesh wound on the fly. In this
apartment, I learned to cut in the bathroom.

I had an ugly bathrobe, cheap velour the color mustard turns when it dries on the rim of the jar. I'd slip the blade, in its little gauze nest, into the bathrobe pocket.

"I'm taking a shower," I'd announce loudly—a touch defiantly?

The hollow-core door shuts behind me. The little button lock clicks into place, and I am, for these few minutes, alone.

I pull the gauze from my pocket, unwrap the blade, lay it on the edge of the sink with a tiny *kchink!* of metal against ceramic. I turn the shower on in subterfuge; licks of steam rise up over the curtain rod.

I prop my leg up on the closed toilet lid, inscribe a careful incision in my thigh. An inch long, or two, but no more. I cut with an infinitesimal slowness that brings the racing speed of my frantic thoughts down and down and down in pitch, like a centrifuge slowing.

The air is thick and wet now. I draw another line next to the first, with half an inch between them. I might dab at the cut with the gauze, a memento of blood I will keep tucked away with the razor. Then I strip my mustard-ugly robe, step into the scalding, scouring heat of the shower, and wash away the evidence in a froth of Clairol's Herbal Essence shampoo.

In the spring, we moved to a new apartment, where I had my own bedroom again. I had my particle-board bed, the slippery blue nylon of my sleeping bag, the green of my lighthouse lamp, and the sweet bite of the razor's edge.

When I think of the history of my cutting, it is this apartment and this bedroom with which I associate it most strongly. I only lived there for about eighteen months, and I cut for the better part of twenty years, so I can't say why this particular setting should resonate most significantly in my memory. Maybe because here was where I perfected the ritual of the act, in the luxury of undisturbed peace.

I always cut at night, hunched on the edge of my bed, illuminated in the ghastly glow of that lamp. Just the anticipation sparked the beginnings of calm. With quiet deliberation I removed the stack of Spanish vocabulary flash cards, unwrapped the blade from its gauze nest, contemplated the precise location for tonight's cut, carefully sterilized my razor with alcohol; when I was through cutting, I swabbed the cut as well, and mopped up the streaks and stains of blood that marked my skin.

I tried one night to cut deeper, torn between the anticipated thrill of a deep slash and the body's organic, mindless resistance to such assault. It wasn't something I put precisely into words, but I knew that I needed to escalate the terms of the engagement. To cut with conviction. To wound for the feverish beauty of the wound itself. I wanted blood—not the refined bubble of sundered capillaries, but a frantic spill, something beyond caution, beyond control.

When I was in sixth grade, a boy in my school, running down the entrance hallway, missed the door handle he'd meant to shove against and instead put his arm through the doorway's glass upper half. It was late in the afternoon, and I was standing outside, waiting for the carpool, when I saw him walking slowly down the sidewalk towards me, holding his right arm out stiffly, staring at it as though mystified. The glass had peeled his arm like a clove of garlic; his forearm was a livid illustration from an anatomy text, muscle wrapped around bone tied with tendon. He trailed a path in scarlet behind him, and when he suddenly sat down, heavily, on the low landscaping wall near where I stood, a velvet pool sprang up beneath him.

"My shoes," he kept saying, "save my shoes," trying to shuffle his feet away from the spreading tide beneath him.

Blood is a color they never get right in the movies. It isn't a flat, ketchupy red. It shimmers with an iridescence underhued in blue. It is the color of living and dying at once, for surely this boy had severed an artery. With every clench of the fist of his heart, more blood arced from his arm in strangely exuberant abandon.

That's what I wanted, that reckless letting go, a moment blind to anything but itself, and the blood. Those delicate cuts that were my stock-in-trade, they were nothing more than a mild protest; I wanted to raise the volume. Desire is unmindful of contingencies or consequences.

I leaned to the left, raised my hand high above the jutting edge of my right hip, willed that hand to drop without thought, to follow the blind law of gravity. Each time, my hand flinched at the last moment. Then finally will overcame body, the blade swept in a swift arc flaying the soft flesh of my hip very nearly to the bone.

Adrenaline washed over me in a tingling rush. I peered into the cut. Bloodless for a moment, as though the vessels and veins and capillaries had been taken by surprise, the waxy white of the fat of my hip looked alien and lifeless. Then blood flooded the wound, ran up and over the edge and rolled along the curve of my hip like rain down a window.

A sudden fear gripped me, a catch deep in the gut; the sides of this wound, unlike all the others before it, gapped open. Had I gone too far? Could I stop the bleeding? What if I needed stitches? There'd be explanations demanded. There'd be consequences.

What had I learned in Red Cross junior lifesaving? I scanned my memory for the proper procedures.

Pressure, I thought. *Apply pressure.*

My fingers pushed the edges of the wound together, and I could see that eventually this would do the trick. I released my hold and studied my fingertips, sticky with blood. Blood streaked my hip and pulsed sluggishly from the wound itself.

My mind trickled back to calm, held in the focus of the moment itself, a futureless, pastless Now. Whatever distresses or anxieties had pushed me to this place, I forgot them all. If you can imagine fighting your way through a howling gale and then stepping into a soundproof room and shutting the door, then I can begin to describe the transition wrought by the stroke of the razor. One moment, chaos; the next, a rich, exquisite silence.

The blood was the essence, the structure of this silence. The size of the cut mattered less than the volume of blood. I had discovered, for instance, that a tiny nick to the ear yielded a surprisingly copious harvest. I found this out when a nurse pricked my ear before I had six teeth pulled in advance of having my braces put on.

"The ear bleeds very easily," she explained to me cheerily, no doubt suffering under the false impression that I might be squeamish, and wanting to distract me, "so we put a little cut here to test how quickly your blood clots."

I tucked away this useful nugget of information and tested it out on some later date. The ear is too visible a body part to resort to on a regular basis without risking discovery, and in the end it leaves no scar either. While the scar mattered less than the blood, still it placed the final seal on each cutting event, and without it I would have been left with an unsatisfactory sense of incompletion.

Nevertheless, an ear bled well, and would keep bleeding generously if I just swiped at the cut with rubbing alcohol to keep it from clotting over. I'd stand in front of the mirror, watching each drop of blood cling to the bottom of my earlobe like the most delicate of earrings, swelling until gravity overcame it and it dripped to my bare shoulder and trickled down across the collarbone. Then I'd smear the blood across my face and chest and stare at the savage, primal face staring at me.

Don't think I don't know how bizarre this sounds. When I've stood thus in front of the mirror, my Narrator has murmured uneasily, *You know, this is very weird.* It created a cognitive dissonance for me; I could never quite reconcile just how weird it was with the rest of my life, one piece of me completely around the bend and the rest of me so unremarkable.

I would stare in that mirror trying to register, to recognize something as my self. I couldn't retain a constant image of myself that was anything like what, intellectually, I thought was probably accurate. Each time I saw my reflection I reacted with a slight mental start of surprise: *This is me? This can't be right.* I'd stare and stare at myself, and the longer I looked the more abstract and unfamiliar that reflection appeared to me. But the blood—that felt tangible. What is more essential than blood? When we speak of the lifeblood of something, we mean its essence, the life at its center. I kept calling upon my blood to prove to me what was my essence.

For a minute, I'd feel I had it pinned down, but as soon as I let the blood thicken and clot, that clarity would begin to trickle from my grasp again, and over days or weeks I would lose it until, with another cut, I could feel I had reclaimed it for another fleeting moment.

Part Two

21

In the spring, I ate a tuna sandwich. I had arrived at this sandwich after ten miserable days of a Mexican holiday with my maternal grandparents, during which time my almost pathological fear of being sick while away from home, combined with our tour guide's chronic warnings of the dire fate awaiting us if we so much as nodded at a piece of fresh fruit, reduced me to a diet of hard rolls and bottled water.

In the airport where my parents came to meet my sister and me on our return, in the cafeteria with the windows overlooking the arriving and departing jets, I ate that tuna fish sandwich with the heartfelt gratitude of a shipwreck survivor, of a condemned man granted a stay of execution. I can remember this sandwich in every detail. It came toasted, on white bread. The tuna was mashed rather than chunky, mixed not with mayonnaise but the sweeter stuff of Miracle Whip, and studded with tiny morsels of pickle relish and bits of boiled egg. Crisp leaves of iceberg lettuce. Out-of-season tomato. Two skewers of toothpick, each tipped by a flourish of curly yellow cellophane. Rippled potato chips on the side. A cold glass of milk.

After nearly two weeks of almost nothing but bread and water, the exquisite variety of taste and texture and flavor in this small feast exploded on me like an incendiary bomb set off in the icy heart of my anorexia. I had given myself permission to eat this sandwich, on the grounds that I had gone so long on so little, and it was this latitude that was my fatal error. Hunger is a crafty negotiator. Once you show the slightest sign of weakness to its honeyed pleas and insinuating manner, it will take this advantage and drive it home, overrunning all your defenses. You can't afford to allow for any hunger at all, or else you find yourself tumbling down that long slippery slope of compromises.

The painstakingly ordered and structured regimen of my eating disorder fell to pieces, crumbling around me like a cliff giving way. It was a terrible kind of bottomless falling, thinking that I would never, ever stop; over the next three years I gained fifty pounds. Although eventually, after much grief and self-recrimination, I would fight my way back down the scale, I would nevertheless never again have anything like a normal relationship with food or body.

It would be tedious to discuss all the dreary vicissitudes entailed by a chronic eating disorder; suffice it to say that the litany of these preoccupations would add a perpetual, keening descant to the clanging chorus already at work in my head.

———————

In that spring of my surrender, I fell hopelessly for one of my sister's brooding, cerebral friends. I've always been vaguely surprised and somehow self-conscious about my own romantic excesses, as though they have represented my failure to live up to a certain ideal of indifference. I could never just have a crush or a casual fancy, it always had to be LOVE in eighteen-point boldface. I could never help myself, it would come on me every time like a sudden case of the flu, and then all I could think about, dream about, care about, was him—whoever the latest him might be.

This particular him returned my affections after a fashion, though he held decided opinions regarding the measured pace and delicate negotiations by which we ought to go about compacting a treaty of our hearts—opinions influenced rather more than I would have preferred by the bloodless counsel of Mr. Spock.

We maneuvered toward each other with the painstaking caution of brain surgery, each step conducted on the high plane of incomprehensible abstraction that was the lingua franca of all my sister's friends. Meanwhile, in my journal, a barely half-candid record written with an eye to an imagined audience, I fretted cautiously under these restraints. When would I see him? When would I talk to him again? When would he kiss me? How I ached for his smile, for a word addressed to me when we were together in a group, for a glancing touch. I dreamed of him for hours, flung across my bed with Simon and Garfunkel playing on my stereo. Under the influence of a Dorothy Sayers murder mystery in which Lord Peter and Harriet Vane solve a murder by breaking a code, I'd taken to writing in my journal in a simple substitution code of mathematical and algebraic symbols. "X^3+UY0" his name read, and it litters that journal like autumn leaves fallen in the yard.

Then one day, late in the spring, I discovered he had gone off to some assignation with another girl. I was talking with a mutual friend on the phone when she innocently let slip the crucial piece of damning information, which on its own meant nothing, but in conjunction with facts already in my possession made the whole story plain.

"I just saw him downtown with Elise," our mutual friend said, when he had expressly and elaborately explained to me how he would be out of town all day with his mother. "He said you were meeting them there."

"Oh, I was going to, but then something came up," I lied. Why was I covering for him when I was the one deceived? Because even in the awful moment of realization, even as one part of me was crushed by this calculated deception, there was another part of me that thrilled to the narrative drama of my new role—the Woman Betrayed.

So this is heartbreak, mused my Narrator. *This should be most interesting.*

This was a wound I didn't want, and yet there was a tantalizing, irresistible awfulness to it, like poking with your tongue at a tooth on the verge of coming out, feeling that raw and bloody emptiness. I probed at it, waiting and waiting to feel the hurt, making a baroque drama for myself in which this new Caroline in her role of love's martyr would be proud, unyielding to any apology or entreaty, insisting that she wanted nothing more to do with him since he had chosen to hold her affections so cheap. Not because she actually felt that way, but because she thought she ought to be someone who could have the self-mastery to put principle over emotion.

I could see how, in the face of this Caroline's continued, steadfast refusal, he would turn at last to the other girl—as he had really, we knew, wanted to do all along—and how Caroline would smile and charm and delight when in their company, never showing the least sign of her broken heart. I saw how he would love the other girl as he had never, we now realized, loved me, how he would laugh with her and adore her and wait longingly for her every word and touch and gesture as I had waited for his. I painted every shade of his love for the other girl in exquisite detail, going over and over each stroke, trying to make it real, trying to make the hurt *my* hurt. But no, I might just as well have been watching my emotions through an observation window.

"Fuck you," I said, and smacked the phone down when he called me, so casual, that evening, but my words were simply what the script called for. *These are the words of an angry person. These are the words an angry person would use,* I had decided.

And when my putative boyfriend called me back, I might just as well have been eavesdropping on someone else's conversation, for all that my words seemed to belong to me. It was as though someone I knew very well were hurt and angry, and sitting in the room with her I could agree that she ought to be hurt and angry, and I was most sympathetic with her hurt and anger, but since it was not *my* hurt and anger all I could suffer was a distress on her behalf, a distress one step removed from the actual experience of that hurt and anger. I watched myself *playing* hurt and anger, and so in this and a hundred, a thousand, other moments I could never keep from suspecting, without ever being able to prove or disprove my suspicions, that my feelings and my behavior at any given time might be entirely fabricated. Shouldn't you be able to know? Shouldn't such things be apparent?

It was as though upsetting events flipped some internal switch, triggering a deadly calm Caroline sent out to negotiate her way through the event with carefully calculated words and responses. Behind her façade, the real crisis flared in a frantic, mounting panic that didn't seem to have anything to do with the actual events unfolding. The scripted Caroline soldiered on with her part, the diversionary tactic, and the other Caroline, provoked by distress, got wound up in a screaming interior altercation that overwhelmed and obliterated anything the external world might throw at me. *Whatareyougoingtodowhatareyougoingtodowhatareyougoingtodo?* shrieked the angry, unruly rabble in my head.

That's when I wanted to tear off my skin and run away from it. That's when I wanted to cut. I cut to quiet the cacophony. I cut to end this abstracted agony, to reel my selves back to one present and physical whole, whose blood was the proof of her tangibility.

22

I spent two years in public school before joyfully abandoning this unloved experiment in egalitarianism—like a nervous gazelle at the watering hole, I'd passed the whole time poised waiting for something terrible to happen to me, waiting to be mugged for my pencils or beaten up in a cafeteria riot. Rumors perpetually abounded of knifings in the bathrooms and robberies in the locker rooms. Of course no one you actually knew had ever experienced or witnessed such things directly, but still the threat lingered in the air like the scent of sour milk in the cafeteria.

The anticipation of a harm that never quite materialized left me in a chronic state of low-level anxiety, a slow drip of a worry. This vague dread, like the ominous rumble of distant thunder, set me perpetually on edge; the fear of an unknown never resolves, because the unknown expands infinitely outward, leaving you to cling pitifully to any small shelter of the known: a cracker has twelve calories; the skin, when cut, bleeds.

Worry is a subject I've had considerable time to explore; I've made something of a life's work of it. I come from a long line of worriers, people with a gift for the lightning-quick calculation of all possible disasters sure to follow any course of action, people who can worry without even having to work at it, who can worry while having fun, who can worry without breaking a sweat. We've raised worry to an art form.

In my family we don't pause when we have lost our train of thought to wonder, *Now what was I thinking about?*, but instead fret, *Now what was I worrying about?*, remembering only the lingering taste of the worry itself. What do we worry about? We worry about everything; there's no matter too great or too insignificant that we can't happily incorporate into the broad reach of our anxieties.

I would never actually have admitted to anyone that I was afraid of school, but with so many people, so many unknowns, who could say what might not happen today or tomorrow or next week? I went to school every day queasy with dread.

I've always been a great believer in the geographic solution: move to a new place or a new love or a new life altogether and leave your troubles behind you like an overlooked suitcase. I don't remember when in the course of ninth grade I first started thinking about boarding school as a possible option for my own life, but it was one of those ideas that catapults from daydream to reality so unexpectedly that you almost can't believe in it. I credit my parents, who (worriers that we are) could have mustered all sorts of reasons why it couldn't be done—chief among these, that we couldn't possibly afford the tuition—but instead encouraged me. In the spring my rescue from public school came in the form of a nice fat scholarship and an invitation from the admissions committee of a girls' school in Richmond, seventy miles away.

In the summer before the beginning, as I saw it, of my new life, I imagined—as I always imagined when I was ready to embark on some kind of starting over—that I would remake myself entirely for the fall. I'd read *The Bell Jar* three times in ninth grade (a suicidal heroine, naturally), and Dorothy Parker, and the farcically outrageous S. J. Perelman, and from their collective influence I cobbled together this idea of a self, someone urbane, implicitly literate, darkly comic. I saw this self as a scandalously outré girl who'd live with a cigarette and a martini in hand (never mind that I couldn't abide tobacco smoke or that martinis were unlikely to be served up with the Tater Tots at family-style dinner in my new school). Of course she would be very skinny, because food bored her, and she would have a raw, ironic urgency about her.

Packing for school, I threw out my razor blades. I wouldn't need them anymore. I would be leaving that self behind for good, in the company of outdated shoes and unwanted record albums. The key in starting over was to walk away from everything that might damn you by association with the former you, with all her defects and drawbacks.

I was just re-reading last year's notebook, I wrote that spring in my journal. *It's so* ridiculous, *the meaningless, irrelevant things I thought were so important! AUGH!*

Every few months or so, I'd start a new journal, in a college-ruled, spiral-bound notebook, its clean white pages my literal tabula rasa. With each new notebook, I'd denounce my most recent former self and her preoccupations, each time declaring my new life to be the new beginning of a higher, better self, who would not be given to such foolishness. I started a new notebook so as to make sure that my new self wasn't contaminated by the drivel and nonsense of that former, lesser me.

Every time, I truly believed that I had indeed begun again, that I had stepped clear and free of everything undesirable about my former self. Then I'd be surprised and dismayed to discover all the unsavory bits and pieces of me that I thought I'd rid myself of, reappearing like a cancer that had metastasized into my new life.

So it was that the sadly familiar and essentially unchanged me arrived at my new school, a plump and bookish scholarship kid with all the wrong clothes. I swear that every other girl in my school was a slender five foot seven, with perfectly blunt-cut, shoulder length hair the color of corn silk, a Fair Isle sweater draped just so across her shoulders, and a delicate gold coil of a belt ringing her neat khaki waist.

In a TV movie, I'd have been destined from the opening credits to torment; I'd have been a lonely outcast sitting miserably alone in my dormitory room on Saturday nights. Fortunately, life is not a television movie.

When I first arrived, I discovered that I would be sharing my dormitory room with three other girls. Ours was the last room on the hall, at the corner of the building, so that we had the advantage of two tall windows. However, we also had two iron bunk beds, four mahogany-laminate bureaus, four closets, two desks, two bookshelves and, in the corner, a small, venerable porcelain sink— all jammed into a surprisingly small cube of space. The paint scheme was that debilitating shade of industrial green, the color of decrepit mental hospitals and police department basements. I was torn between a resolute determination to be happy about everything at my new school (I feared doubt; to allow even one misgiving would be to risk burial under an avalanche of them), and a sinking dismay at the thought of spending the next nine months shoehorned into this unprepossessing space with these three girls.

I didn't like feeling encroached upon by the chaos of their stuff, their talk, their musical taste and their shampoo bottles and their sweaters flung across the furniture. So, over the coming weeks, without being obvious about it, I confined myself to those spaces I had staked out as mine alone: my closet, my bureau, my top bunk on the bed. I had to tuck each thing of mine safely within these protected zones. I wouldn't put my books in the shared shelves or my record albums in the communal pile or let my sweaters mingle with the others. In the opening weeks of school I suffered painfully from homesickness; as an antidote, somehow each of my things served as a sacred vessel through which Home was embodied within the walls of my dormitory room. These vessels could be contaminated, lose their power of embodiment, in contact with all the otherness in this room. I can't quite define what I feared—perhaps the disintegration of my coherent self.

Nevertheless I got along with all my roommates, because I almost always get along. I am masterly at sidestepping conflict and avoiding dissent. If I can find common ground, however narrow and tenuous, I will stake it out. I mold myself to the shape that suits the situation. I can't remember quite what role I assumed amid my three completely unlike roommates. Generic teenager, I believe, is the position I took. Talk about boys and clothes and hair and parties—girls'-hut stuff—though of clothes and hair and parties I knew virtually nothing, and of boys I thought it best to keep much of what I knew discreetly to myself. Like a deep-cover spy, however, I could wing the colloquialisms in the foreign language of girlness, and by this means get along.

I suppose I could have kept it up all year, but as it turned out attrition was on my side. Within six weeks two of my roommates had left school, one running away and the other yanked home by parents feuding through a bitterly contentious divorce, and that left only two of us to enjoy what had now become a conversely voluminous space. My remaining roommate was a high-spirited party girl who occasionally smoked dope in the closet and made me feel unexpectedly sheltered and naive with her outrageous tales of sex and drinking in her beachfront hometown, and though we appeared to have almost nothing in common, nevertheless we hit it off as well as you might hope for a roommate. I let myself, at last, spread out into my new life.

My new school was nothing like the one where I'd grown up. It sat on a long rectangle of campus smack in the heart of a rarefied Richmond neighborhood of brick colonials and Georgian revivals, with the requisite stately oaks and patiently nurtured boxwoods. It was very much a place for the Southern daughters of Southern daughters, among whom I found myself once again the Token Yankee, but it was no mere finishing school. We were expected to live up to the school's long tradition of intellectual rigor, and to do our educators proud in the college admissions sweepstakes.

I rose to the bait, and applied myself to my academic life as one pursued by demons. I perpetually aspired to be one of those girls who rose at seven, after a full and restful night's sleep, and consequently arrived at morning chapel an hour later bathed and coiffed and looking like an incarnation of the L. L. Bean catalogue, with her books and her papers tidily arranged.

Instead all I ever managed was to perfect the art of last-minute miracles, from bolting out of bed three minutes short of the morning's first required attendance to cramming for tests and whipping out papers in bleary all-nighters commenced at ten o'clock on the evening before the due date.

I did everything the wrong way. My clothes were forever rumpled and my collars grubby and no matter how I tied and retied them my crew-neck sweaters never draped artfully across my imperfect and slouching shoulders. I studied in a messy heap amid the tangled linens and blankets of my never-made bunk bed (rather than, as our study skills manuals advised, with two feet planted firmly on the floor, sitting upright at a neatly organized desk with a good reading lamp). I committed vast sums of information to memory on the night before a test, and promptly forgot all of it the minute I'd answered the last question.

It's not that I didn't love learning. It's just that there was learning, and then there was the game of academics, which was another matter altogether, one where measurement was all.

I began with the goal of placing out of tiresome required evening study hall with the necessary 3.5 or better average on a 4.0 scale. Then I got to liking all those delicate intervals between 3.5 and 4.0: the earnest 3.6, the cheeky 3.7, the proud 3.8, the ambitious 3.9, and at last the pristine perfection of the 4.0. Below 3.5 oozed a great, sucking morass, and if a quiz or an assignment came back to me marked with a 3.2 or a 3.4, I could feel the dark waters of failure licking at my ankles. Below 3.5 we were sinking into the nether regions of the B's, and let's face it: A B− is just a C+ on borrowed time.

My GPA was only one in a series of numerical value systems in which I invested my faith. I found numbers comfortingly tangible and reliable: weight on the scale, sit-ups counted off, dollars in a savings account. You could dispute the *relative* value of any given number—a 3.5 versus a 3.6, say, or fifty minutes' exercise as opposed to an hour's worth—but you couldn't dispute the numbers themselves. Counting up or counting down, you could rely on numbers to order themselves in neat hierarchies against which you could measure your progress in the world.

My GPA was magical to me. It had the power to confirm or refute my worth. It had the power to shape my present and determine my future. However, I saw my academic success as the thinnest possible veneer laid over my otherwise doubtful underpinnings, as if I were a car-lot lemon running just long enough to dupe an unsuspecting buyer. When you took away the GPA, what was left? At any moment I might blow the whole gig and fall irredeemably from grace. I already felt depressed in anticipation of the event. The Very Good College of all my hopes and dreams shimmered like a Shangri-La on my personal horizon, and now my entire fate, I believed, turned on each grade. One disastrous paper, one quiz blown, and you could kiss the Ivy League good-bye. I couldn't have articulated which specific, disastrous consequences I expected to result from failure to gain admission to a first-ranked New England college—the contingency was simply too unthinkable in itself. I could just feel a whole future evaporating.

But when your report cards reflect an unsullied sweep of 3.7's and 3.9's, then you can steep in the warm bath of esteem from teachers, parents, fellow students.

We are very proud of your success, wrote my father in a letter to me.

You are on your way towards being one of their best students, wrote my mother.

When, I wondered, would I fuck up?

One night in my junior year—a night when, unusually, I actually went to bed at a reasonable eleven P.M.—I began, as I lay in bed in the darkness, to tremble. At first just a quick shudder, the kind you have when something sets you briefly on edge—a spider dashing over your foot, the sound of fingernails on a blackboard. Then another shudder. Then another and another, and then I couldn't stop. Waves of uncontrollable trembling, one after the other. I tried breathing deeply. I tried willing my muscles to relax. Still I continued to shake. It started to scare me; I thought I must be on the verge of some terrible illness. Something awful was going to happen to me, and I was so far from home. The more anxious I got, of course, the worse I shook. Finally I couldn't stand it anymore. I called out to my roommate. I said, "Something's wrong, I can't stop shaking."

She turned on the light and sat up.

"You what?" she said.

"I can't stop shaking," I repeated, trembling violently.

"Are you sick?"

"I don't know."

"Should I get somebody?"

"I don't know."

She watched me shuddering and twitching, but perfectly lucid and conscious.

"I'll go get Lucy," she said, finally, naming the dorm counselor on the floor above us who was casual and unflappable and someone you could trust in a crisis.

"Okay," I said shakily.

She came back in a few minutes with Lucy, who sat down on the edge of my bed and put a comforting arm on my shaking body.

"What's wrong?" she said.

"I don't know," I said again.

"Do you think you're sick?"

"I don't know."

I explained how I'd just been lying there, and started shaking and couldn't stop. I said I didn't feel sick or feverish or anything, but still I couldn't stop.

Lucy fetched a thermometer—no fever. She sat me up and wrapped me in a blanket. Still I trembled. She went and roused my own dorm counselor, Janet, who lived with her husband in a tiny apartment on our floor. Janet, bathrobed and hair in curlers, stood with Lucy, both of them examining me critically as though they were sizing up a thoroughbred with questionable parentage or an artwork with a dubious provenance.

We went through all the questions again. Was I sick? Had I taken something? Had I gotten too hot or too cold? Had I hurt myself somehow?

"Let's go to my apartment," said Janet at last. "Maybe Bob can help." Bob was her husband who, I happened to know, was studying for his master's in psychology. Bob was stretched out in a lounger in their cubicle of a living room watching Johnny Carson. Johnny and Ed exchanged witticisms. Janet wrapped me in an afghan crocheted in the browns and reds and golds of the seventies. Bob quizzed me with probing questions. Had I been under any particular stress? A test hanging over me? A paper due? Was there anything else in my life that might be troubling me?

Stress, I'd admit to. Stress sounded good, better than all the mysterious, doctors-would-scratch-their-heads, sudden-onset fatal illnesses I'd been imagining for the past twenty minutes. And stress you could qualify for with ordinary kinds of problems; you didn't have to prove any major mental disorders.

"Maybe I've just gotten myself a little tired out lately," I suggested.

Bob reached down to the coffee table and picked up a small, curved white plastic object with a shiny chrome plate at one end. It was about the size of a woman's electric razor. I had no idea what to make of it.

"Put this in your hand and put your thumb on the metal part," Bob instructed.

I held it in my hand and placed my thumb on the metal pad. The instrument let out a high-pitched electronic wail.

"It's a biofeedback device," explained Bob. "It's measuring

tension. You concentrate on lowering the pitch and volume and that makes you relax."

Oh, I thought to myself, interested, still shaking like an aspen in high wind.

I sat there. The biofeedback instrument went slowly from shriek to whine to hum, and the trembling subsided with it. Bob continued watching Carson. Janet bustled around somewhere in the background. After a while I began to feel self-conscious and awkward with my humming thumb, sitting in their living room, their private space, imposing myself on their off-duty lives. I had caused such a to-do over nothing. Was my stress any more stressful than anyone else's? We all had schoolwork. We all stayed busy. It was probably my own fault, anyway, for putting off everything until the night before it was due.

Unsure how best to extricate myself, finally I just stood up and folded the afghan and said, "Well thanks, I guess I'll be going now. Sorry to have kept you up so late."

Janet popped her head around the doorway. "You're sure you're okay now?"

"Oh, I'm fine, really, I mean I'm sorry I bothered you-all with me just stressing out like this." I was oozing toward the doorway, bowing and scraping and apologizing all the way.

I crept back into my room, where my roommate was asleep, and back into my bed, and lay there for a while, wondering, *What was that all about?*

$2\mathcal{S}$

There was a family pharmacy nicknamed Doc's next door to my school, with a drugstore soda fountain where women with cat-eye glasses and beehive hairdos made BLTs and limeades. The fast girls from school hung out on a brick wall behind Doc's, smoking cigarettes and drinking Tab and talking the fast-girl talk of parties and drinking and sex.

Doc's was where we went for life's necessities like toothpaste, and last-minute greeting cards to send for a grandmother's birthday, and tampons that I stood in line with, praying that it wouldn't be the owner's teenage son ringing me up when it came time to pay.

I was waiting in line there one afternoon, maybe three months into my first year at boarding school. The last of the autumn leaves were blowing in a dank November wind, and first-trimester exams loomed in the coming weeks. I had not yet fully overcome homesickness, and when I walked every day through the quarter-mile of neighborhoods to our brother school down the street, where I took Spanish III, third period, and made my laborious way through verb conjugations and translating the *Poema del Cid,* the warm lights spilling from the windows of the cozy little Cape Cods hunkered down against the morning chill made me lonely for the normal life I'd never really had.

So I was standing in line at Doc's that afternoon, idly studying the rows of last-minute purchases shelved neatly behind the counter, when my eyes strayed across a little box labeled "Wilkinson Bond." It was a very sweet and neat little box, like a tiny envelope, maybe two inches long and a quarter-inch thick. It was set amongst a variety of different sorts of razors and blades, so I knew what it must be.

"And could you add a box of those Wilkinson Bond?" I asked, as casually as possible, as my purchases were rung up. My heart pounded as I waited in dread for the woman behind the counter to demand to know what I needed those razors for. Could my history be read on my face?

But no, she popped the box into the bag with my toothpaste and my shampoo without even a second glance.

I walked back to my dorm with the brown paper bag clutched close to my chest, strangely comforted by the knowledge of that small package inside, yet expecting to be stopped at any moment by a teacher, a dorm counselor. I might as well have been smuggling a fifth of gin back to my dorm room, for the furtive manner in which I scuttled up the back stairway and shoved the bag into the back of my underwear drawer.

What did I expect? That my English teacher would run across me and say, "What have you got in the bag, Caroline? Razor blades for cutting yourself up?"

At the moment of purchasing them, if you can believe me, I didn't really think it was my intention to use them for what, in my sense, was their obvious purpose. I'm not sure what else I might have thought I was going to do with them. The fact is that I didn't really think at all, I asked for the box out of impulse, thinking it was so exquisitely small and rectangularly proportioned and desirable. It didn't occur to me that there was something decidedly odd in finding a box of razor blades aesthetically appealing. I wonder if a heroin addict loves the elegant simplicity of the needle, if a drinker romances the curve and shape of the bottle.

During study hall that night, safely alone—and how could I not have understood that if I waited for solitude, then something was certainly afoot?—I drew the box from the bag stored carefully in my drawer. What delight in finding that each rectangle of a blade came wrapped in its own neatly creased, crisp alabaster square of translucent waxed paper! Unlike the narrow sliver of a blade snapped from a disposable Bic, which had to be held pinchingly by fingertips, this new blade was large enough to grasp comfortably, and rested lightly, easily in the hand. It would skim across skin with the delicacy of the sheerest wisp of drapery stirred in the window by a warm evening's breeze.

I had to know it now, how this blade would sing its own clear note upon my skin. Only once, I said to myself. Then only once more, because yes, how fine was the swift flicker of its passage! The perfect congress of skin and blade, and the elegant, industrial-age precision of the cut. Like the letting-go of a long-held breath, like the first deep draught of cool water on a parched throat.

I needed cutting now the way a diabetic needs insulin. It was a bulwark, steady and unyielding, I could throw up against the insidious, corrosive lapping of a whispering sea of uneasiness.

————

It's surprising how easy it is to get away with self-mutilation, as long as you do your cutting with a measure of self-restraint. If someone notices a cut on your arm or your thigh—even a couple of cuts—what cognitive leap would have to be made to conclude that those wounds had been self-inflicted? Particularly when there's no other evidence to indict your stability. Everyone knows the signs of a troubled teen, right? Losing interest in school, poor grades, hanging around with the wrong crowd. Loud music. Drugs maybe, or drinking. Acid-rocker T-shirts.

We believe so strongly in the face value of things. What would there have been about me, with my honor-roll standing and my respectable cross-section of friends and the wordplays I tossed into our English-class vocabulary quizzes, to have suggested any cause for alarm?

24

I had a boyfriend, a most coveted item in boarding school, who was one among our theater crowd. He was the first boyfriend with whom I actually went on a date. We ate at Pizza Hut. We saw movies and shared popcorn. We made out in his fifteen-year-old Chevrolet with the passenger door that never opened, Fleetwood Mac playing on the eight-track.

Look at me, mused my Narrator. *Parking! How novel! How charmingly American teenager!*

My boyfriend was devoted to me; I blew most of every evening's study hours talking on the phone with him, and we spent every minute that we could together, and after a while I let my guard down.

Lucky him. Degree by degree I fell apart on him, letting the chaotic Caroline crawl out and go to pieces in the middle of our dates—which I seemed to regard as a kind of shore leave from my public self. In the womb of that old Chevrolet, in a certain kind of desperate mood, I sometimes sank into a nearly catatonic state, curled up in a fetal ball on the worn vinyl of the front seat, mute to my boyfriend's entreaties. I could feel myself moving farther and farther away, watching this Caroline with her arms wound tight around her legs, and for twenty minutes or a half an hour or more it seemed impossible that she might ever unwrap herself from this paralysis.

At other times I broke down in hysterical, hyperventilating sobs, with no forewarning or subsequent explanation.

"What's wrong?" he'd beg. "Tell me what's wrong."

"I don't know," I'd say. "I don't know," and I honestly didn't know.

I even told him, eventually, about the cutting, though in a cautious bit of PR I couched it in the past tense.

"I used to cut myself with razor blades," I said, pointing to the ghostly scars on my arms. Still he did not forsake me.

Outside the shelter of the Chevrolet, however, I dedicated myself to maintaining for everyone else the impression of irreverent insouciance. I cast myself as the comically maladroit figure at the heart of one tale of misadventure after another. Humor at your own expense allows you great latitude. I'd vent my anxieties by making jokes of them.

"The average family has two-point-five children," I'd say. "My sister's the point-five and I'm the other two." Or, when I had some trouble reaching my parents by telephone, "My family's given me up for Lent."

I played comedy much better than tragedy. This capering Caroline was like the sidekick in a half-hour sitcom, there to leaven the plot with ironic asides, the comic relief if ever things threatened to turn grave.

The more devotedly I built this image, the more impossibly difficult it seemed to imagine admitting anything else. I felt I had a responsibility. People were relying on me to be the steady course, the home light burning in the window, the oatmeal when too much rich dining has taxed the taste buds. I wanted to live up to that responsibility. I wanted to be the kind of person about whom people would say, "You know, you can always rely on her."

Was that apparent me less than a true self? I don't know. Did her dissociation from my inner life make her only a fabrication? I don't know. In some respects, she felt the most true, the way she refused to take things too seriously, the way she could see the absurd in the worst moments. I found falling back upon her a relief. She made her way almost easily through the world, got along with everyone, covered well for all my insecurities and uncertainties, and though sometimes her flippancy was like a nervous tic offered up, to my occasional regret, before I took time to think better of her words, for the most part she pretended for me the confidence I didn't feel. She would brush off the setbacks that incapacitated me. She enjoyed life. I would have been happy to be her.

25

If I tell you now that I had a great time at boarding school, that I count it still among the best three years of my life, does that make sense? For those three years, every day had purpose. I could wake up and feel that I was moving forward with my life, with a steady accumulation of academic honors, with goals to meet, with college to aspire to, with satisfying accomplishments to mark my progress. I could point to these things and say, *These define me.*

By my senior year, even the cool girls had extended their camaraderie to me, inviting me to the cool parties—though I wouldn't have had any idea what to say or do at a cool party. The point, however, was that I'd been invited. I had arrived. I had climbed the pinnacle of high school success. I had my hand in a dozen extracurriculars and my name on a letter of admission from my first-choice college. Had a new boyfriend (the old one having gone off to college and a mutual parting of the ways) who wrote me cerebral mash notes while we analyzed the blood-spattered passion of Federico García Lorca in Spanish V. I'd even almost managed a miracle makeover, shedding those extra pounds, getting my braces off and contact lenses on. My senior year was one big bang-up success, anticipated to culminate in the prep school version of the Rapture, the day on which I would ascend to that Very Good New England College of all my hopes and aspirations.

"I'm searching for my destiny," I sang in my solo in the Freshman Revue, gazing wistfully into the upper balcony. I'd sung alto in high school chorale, and "alto" was what I wrote on my audition sheet for the revue, but after I sang for the musical auditionist he said to me, "You know, you're really a contralto."

And I thought, "Wow, this is college. It's not just four-part harmony anymore."

Then I promptly ran out of steam.

I had no sense of purpose in college. I'd spent the last three years focused on the ultimate goal of Getting into a Good College. I'd never particularly considered what ought to happen beyond that goal. Where was life supposed to go from here? What was the point, really, of college? Was it career preparation? Four years to kill before you were forced to concede to adulthood? Four years to devote to broadening the mind and expanding intellectual horizons? Four years of beer parties and casual sex?

I didn't know what I ought to do, and I didn't even know how to begin to figure out what I ought to do. I'd just followed the expected path: gradeschoolhighschoolcollege. So now what? I was expected to make decisions for myself, decisions on which a future I couldn't even envision would be built. How could I decide how to prepare myself when I had no idea what I was preparing for?

So I went on living for my GPA because it was something you could count on, the A that says you're okay, the B like a red light flashing, warning DANGER! TROUBLE AHEAD!, the C and below unspeakable, unmentionable, unimaginable.

All the confidence I'd left high school with evaporated at my beautiful, ivy-covered New England college, where I was thrown into a crowded little pool where *everyone* was a former high school star, where my nothing little vita from my nobody's-heard-of-it prep school seemed paltry and irrelevant in comparison to all those utterly accomplished graduates of Exeter and Andover and Choate. It wasn't that I didn't think I had abilities. I just assumed, in spite of whatever accomplishments I had thus far managed in life, that everyone I would be competing with would always be that much more accomplished, and confident as well, and would wear the right clothes, and would actually be able to remember what "ontological" means.

I couldn't help feeling that even English, my chosen course of study, represented a major by default, rather than some bold, challenging choice by means of which I would set the world on fire. All my friends seemed to be choosing the exotic (philosophy, religion, anthropology) or the controversial (economics, political science) or the cerebral (mathematics, astronomy), and here I was reading Wordsworth again, just as in my junior year in high school.

Pinning everything on my GPA invested it with way, way too much importance. I got a D once on a short paper, a one-pager I'd tried to be much too clever with, and I spent the rest of the day seriously considering killing myself over it. Suicide! Over some crappy one-pager for a course I can't even call to mind anymore.

Well, imagine having to live with that Caroline day in and day out. You might be inclined to go for the razor, too, just to shut her up.

26

For lack of more productive things to do with my time, what I did with college was run through boyfriends the way a chain-smoker burns through cigarettes.

I liked falling in love. It was like a drug. A rush of pure, un-intellectualized, unexamined feeling, in all its untarnished newness. For those first few weeks, when you are both on your best behavior and the heady delights of novelty have not yet worn away, what could be more exhilarating? I'd put aside school, friends, sleep, eating, take up his interests, hang out with his friends, maybe even consider his major or sign up for a course he'd approve of. It was pathetic.

I lacked endurance for the long haul, however. That brief flame of passion dwindled soon enough to embers, then to ashes. I would sink again into emptiness, and blame him for the sinking. He wasn't quite what I'd hoped he would be. Too much that or too little this. Too possessive or too aloof. Too arrogant or too insecure. And then somehow I'd find myself wrapped in someone else's passionate embrace, without ever having officially severed relations with the old guy. I'd imagine the painful, awkward, unpleasant scene of an official breakup. The anger. The recriminations. I couldn't bring myself to face it—why precipitate so much suffering? Wasn't it easier just to let things die quietly away in a hint here, a sign there? I'd let him drift along in ignorance of my betrayal until my distant manner and possibly a most obvious attachment to my new fancy made the picture plain.

I had just low enough an opinion of myself to be able to rationalize each time that the ex was probably relieved anyway. Once I was over any one of these boys it seemed hard to imagine that he wasn't equally over me—I still can't quite convince myself that anyone has ever loved me enough to be sorry when I was gone.

I didn't set out to deceive. I don't think that I really recognized, even in the midst of it, that it *was* a deception. I'd spent long enough living by the proposition that people were happier when they knew less that editing no longer seemed like deception to me. After burning down the house, however, there's no point in saying that hadn't been your intention when you lit the match.

So what I got out of college were squirmingly uncomfortable memories of half a dozen people I can dread running into at reunions.

———

My first two years of college were a blur of boyfriends that reached its sorry denouement in a beer-sodden midwinter fling with a recently deposed boyfriend's best friend visiting for the weekend from home.

Sophomore year was a terrible year, with the novelty of freshman year behind us and the long grind of three years until graduation still ahead. It rained all fall. The New England winter arrived early and left late, without even a decent measure of snow to make it charming; our Winter Carnival took place in a sea of squelching mud under overcast skies. Day after day dawned to a lusterless winter light, the sky as washed out and featureless as an old rag.

The liaison with the best friend from home unfolded in the dead heart of January. It was our Winter Study term, one month dedicated to focused study of a single, nontraditional course. Leaving large swathes of unoccupied time for remaining holed up in your dormitory, out of the cold, dispirited weather, drinking Bloody Marys with your suitemates while the dirty sky surrendered to darkness at four o'clock.

On this particular evening I'd had just enough beer to depress me, at just another in the endless series of keg parties that strung the days of Winter Study together, and I sat there too indifferent to move while he wooed me with a dime-store seduction.

"Long hair is so sexy on a woman," he murmured, his fingers tangling in the waist-length fall of mine.

"This party is boring," he whispered. "Isn't there someplace we could go?"

Oh, please, did he get this stuff off the inside of a matchbook cover? my Narrator demanded from a distance made even greater by the disorienting effect of the beer, but still I went along with a dull resignation, like the condemned mounting the gallows knowing it's pointless to resist.

I just sighed to myself, *Oh, why not.* At that moment I didn't even care enough anymore to bother extricating myself.

In the whey-light of another winter dawn, I sat sleepless on my bed, feeling the preceding night's unctuous improprieties like a greasy residue on my flesh. My life repulsed me. I was stumbling along from one boy to the next without even bothering anymore to justify it to myself, like the addict who can't see, doesn't care, beyond the next high, trying to hold on to a feeling—any feeling—

that would nevertheless slip away like water trickling through fingers.

"You're out of control!" one of my suitemates had hissed at me only a day before.

I was so tired, so discouraged, and I wanted to free myself of my self the way a snake divests itself of its skin.

I took my razor blade—my handy razor blade, my dear and trusted and always reliable razor blade—and started at my elbow. An inch, two inches, it didn't seem like enough. Three, four inches, the razor crept down the length of my arm, with the faint *tthick tthick* of its slow passage audible. I got to my wrist, and watched the way the blood faded in, at first so faint that I could wonder if I was really seeing anything at all, then a precise thread of crimson that almost as soon as it appeared began to differentiate into a hundred individual beads.

Not quite. Try again.

Starting maybe a quarter-inch from the first cut, I drew a second line down my arm in perfect parallel. Elbow to wrist.

Now what? Two long, lonely lines. Too much imbalance on the winter-white canvas of my arm. I cut a third line, again a quarter-inch from the second. A fourth. A fifth. I scored my way, line by line, around the entire circumference of my forearm.

Do you know what? It was exciting, in a low, dangerous kind of way. It was darkly satisfying in its excess. Every additional line was like one more step away from caution and discretion. By the sixth or seventh or eighth long cut, a fiery warmth spread up my arm, and it was the heat of conflagration and exorcism.

I cut with painstaking, deliberate slowness and a mounting sense of—excitement? Anticipation? Expecting to cross, at last, some final threshold, to realize some permanent escape. A blood sacrifice substantive enough to articulate the depth and breadth and conviction of my despair.

But when I was done, and I sat with my ravaged, seeping,

stinging arm propped awkwardly on its elbow in front of me, all I could think was, *This is not enough.* It occurred to me, for the first time in all these years of cutting, that no cut ever would be enough. Linearity was a cheap illusion—there was no moving forward with life, no upward, onward, outward: it was all just the same endless repetition. You washed your hair today, but tomorrow it would just need washing again. You made a stupid mistake today, and tomorrow you'd make another.

As if to bear out this conclusion, that night I had the inspired idea to thrust my scabbed-over arm in front of another recently-ex-boyfriend. After years of hiding a hundred inconsequential little scratches and cuts, this was the moment when I chose to reveal myself as a self-mutilator in full sail, with my arm a garish plow zone of bloody furrows.

Wordlessly, I swept back my flannel shirtsleeve with suitable flourish, expecting I don't know what. I hadn't made the cuts with the idea that I was going to parade them around for public delectation, and yet it's hard not to suspect that there was something calculated in my decision to show this, my most extreme gesture of self-mutilation, when I had kept so many other incidents secret. What did I hope to gain? Was I looking for absolution? Was I hoping the severity of my self-excoriations would win me a kind of Chapter 11 from those I had sinned against, setting me free of my emotional debts?

Whatever I was expecting, it wasn't his actual response, which was simply to stare at me in horror.

"My God, what did you do to yourself?" he said, recoiling as though I had ripped open my chest and thrown my still-beating heart on the floor in front of him.

In a movie this scene would have gone much better. A dramatic confrontation, or a weeping confession, or a jump-cut to the psych-ward scene. *Something.* Instead, I just stood there dumbfounded. *What did I do to myself?* Wasn't that obvious? Did I really need to spell it out?

"Um, I just . . . it's only . . . I mean . . . I mean, it's no big deal," I mumbled, yanking my sleeve down, backing out of the doorway of his dormitory room, turning to flee down the hall. He made no effort to pursue.

Here was the upshot of the whole business: A few evenings later, my ex-with-the-best-friend-from-home sauntered by my room, beer in hand and probably a few down the hatch as well. I don't remember his precise words, but in a disturbingly cheery voice, as though he were telling a highly amusing story, he took me to task for my entire sorry performance since the (regrettable) day he'd met me, and then conjectured broadly on my probable lapses of the past and all that might unfortunately be anticipated of me in a similar vein in the future. I stood there trembling, silent, wanting to defend myself and yet having to concede miserably to myself the essential justice of his words. Regardless of its intentionality—or, more precisely, its lack thereof—my behavior *was* execrable and indefensible.

In the end, before throwing his half-empty beer over me as a parting gesture, he made one final accusation that I do remember specifically:

"You just talk about your cutting as a spiel to get guys," he said.

Putting aside the question of whether self-mutilation could be considered a complement to even the most perverse of seductions, we come to the more puzzling issue raised by his accusation: that clearly I had told him about the cutting, and moreover that he obviously didn't think himself to be the sole recipient of such confidences.

How would I have brought it up? What would I have said? I can't begin to imagine how I would have broached the subject amid the murmured exchange of lovers' intimacies. Did I hope to paint myself as poetically tragic and therefore fitting my own odd idea of desirable? Why is it that I can't remember these conversations, either in general or in particular? Memory is faithless, like a cheating lover, telling you what you believe is true.

———

Everything led to nothing. Winter Study came to an end and another semester started and I wore long sleeves for a few weeks, until the scabs had given way to barely visible, thin white scars.

I can no longer tell if I have/had real emotional troubles or if it is/was merely melodrama, I wrote in my journal, genuinely uncertain, as always, of the truth or fiction of my own feelings.

27

I've always believed that immediately upon throwing something away you will discover this discarded item to be the one thing you need above all others. After my Winter Study wounding, in yet another fit of resolve, I'd thrown out all my razor blades. Thus, when I decided, that spring, that what I needed was to kill myself, I was razorless for the job.

As with the other times I'd come to this psychic brink, I felt as though I was trying to solve a problem in the present rather than getting rid of myself for good. Once again, I wanted to kill something *in* myself, wanted to bleed it out until I was left with the bare, clean baseline, the absolute zero from which point I could rebuild a better version of myself.

The catalyst for this particular low moment was a falling-out with my suitemates, women I'd started the year with in happy camaraderie. We were college sophomores, brimming with confidence and pleasure in our wisdom of the world.

The manic course of my personal life over the intervening months had strained our friendship to the snapping point.

"What the hell are you doing with yourself?" one of them demanded at last, confronting me in the stretch of hall that linked our individual rooms. I had, I think, some boy in tow at the moment.

"What do you mean?" I said hotly, embarrassed to be thus taken to task with my latest fancy—oh hell, he wasn't even a fancy, I hardly even *knew* him, he was just a nanosecond's distraction—standing by my side: the evidence of my crimes.

"You're making a mess of your life," she warned, and of course she was right, but the upshot of this confrontation was a furtive, slinking, mutual avoidance.

It was four o'clock, the suicide hour. It seemed like more effort than I could ever imagine undertaking to walk across campus to the drugstore for more blades. No doubt I'd run into someone I knew, and have to carry on a conversation. How can you carry on a conversation when you're getting ready to go kill yourself? It's always the damn ordinary getting in the way like that.

Instead, I decided I would break a juice glass I'd carried up to my room one night after dinner, and get myself a nice jagged piece for the dirty work. My plan was to break the glass by throwing it at the solid, fire-impervious door to my bedroom. I was all caught up in the cinematic drama of the event. I could anticipate already the satisfying *pop!* of the shattering glass and the sudden snow of broken shards upon my floor.

This is anger, I thought, nevertheless feeling all too theatrical as I let loose with the first pitch, hurling it at the door.

It bounced unharmed to the floor and rolled under my desk.

After I'd crawled under my desk to retrieve it again for the fourth or fifth time, the afternoon's drama began losing some of its focus.

Self-consciousness kept checking the force of my throw; what were my suitemates going to think? The sound of the glass ricocheting off the door was startlingly loud. Would they come and demand to know what I was up to? Wouldn't I feel foolishly melodramatic trying to explain? *Yeah, I'm trying to break a glass. I'm either planning to kill myself, or deluding myself into thinking I'm planning to kill myself, but I'm not sure which. Check back with me tomorrow, and if I'm dead, then we'll know.*

I had it all worked out so that Al, our tireless and nearly toothless custodian, would be minimally inconvenienced. Al had always been a great help to us, bringing the vacuum cleaner around when we needed it and assuring us we were all very nice girls and he could tell us he'd seen some troublemakers in his time. I thought it would be the height of arrogance to leave some godawful mess, another case of the privileged college kids sticking it to the help. So I was going to sit on the floor, with my bleeding wrists propped up over the trash can in front of me. How much blood do you lose before your heart ceases to pump out any more? Certainly not a wastebasket's full, and since the wastebasket was lined with a plastic bag, not even a rinse would be required.

This was my way of going about suicide—getting all caught up in the logistics and the technical details while overlooking the essential issue that suicide was about being dead.

Did I mean to kill myself? I understand that when you really mean to kill yourself, you're so relieved by having made the decision for good that you're very nearly cheerful. I'd say what I felt that afternoon was more like a bustling efficiency, as if I were a home handyman readying for a project. Maybe I just wanted to test the limits of my despair, to see how far I was willing to go to get away from myself.

The glass broke, at last. I scratched at my arm, but the cruelly pointed shard felt as crude as a bludgeon. It had none of the simple beauty of the razor's edge. A razor blade slips between cells the way water insinuates itself through rock, finding the path that is there. I could see already that the whole thing was going to be a write-off.

I probably never could have gone quite so far as to kill myself anyway, not while any assignments remained pending: let not my epitaph read "She missed the due date." My Hi-Liter bobbed unsinkable through every crisis. Papers were turned in on time, I showed up more or less reliably for class, I appeared on schedule for my financial aid job, dutifully typing up schedules and team rosters for the athletic department. Academics just rolled on, as inevitable as the sun rising in the morning, and it never occurred to me that I could fail to continue rolling along with them. They were the bus I couldn't get off.

I made over the afternoon's fiasco into my next assignment for Advanced Fiction Workshop. The way I saw it, my whole life might be a fiction anyway—who knew?—so I might just as well mine it for twenty pages double-spaced.

The next day I went down to the pharmacy and bought myself a new package of Wilkinson-Bond. Then I was like the smoker joyfully abandoning another attempt at quitting, settling back for that first starved drag sucked down to the cellular level.

28

The winter of that sophomore year, my oracular suitemate had predicted, "You'll marry a fellow student right out of school, and then you'll get divorced, because you rushed into the marriage thinking you could find happiness and perfection there."

Actually I waited an entire year before marrying, but that's only because my future ex-husband was a year behind me. He was the son of working-class Cape Codders, whose family had lived generations on the peninsula.

In high school and two years of community college he had worked at the A&P where his father was manager, and suffered the summer people who looked through him unless they wanted his help finding the maraschino cherries or the gherkins. Now he found himself classmate to almost an entire school's worth of the equivalent of summer people—people accustomed to a familiar and easy relationship with money—and he couldn't help but feel that somehow he was betraying his loyalties and sleeping with the enemy. The two of us had in common, we used to remark to each other only half in jest, that we were educated beyond our station in life.

When we met, we were terribly pleased to discover so much that we had in common, we who both felt never quite at home, who always had one foot in some real or imagined other life. Like me, he didn't know what he wanted or ought to do with his life, or who he ought to be. Like me, he relied in the meantime on his GPA to stand for himself. Like me, he was a dedicated procrastinator. Like me, he was driven by a merciless and unsympathetic Inner Yankee who demanded, *Downplay your troubles and get on with it.* Like me, he found irony as comfortingly familiar as an old sweater.

Like me, I say. Like me. We wouldn't have believed it then, but eventually we would discover that it's possible to have too much in common.

———

In the winter of his senior year, after we'd ruled out what we thought were all the reasons why we shouldn't, we decided to marry. That's how we put it to everyone:

"We couldn't come up with any other reasons not to get married," we said.

Of course, we knew plenty of reasons, reasons that gnawed away at us, unspoken. I know we both suspected the truth we would soon discover: that we were marrying each other not out of a passionate commitment to mutual lifelong devotion, but because we were so overwhelmed at the prospect of having to go out into the world and construct a life for ourselves that we couldn't imagine how to do it alone.

I think we half hoped someone else would give us a reason to change our minds, would put a foot down where we couldn't.

"Do you think we shouldn't get married?" I asked my friends, my co-workers. Everyone thought it was just prewedding jitters. Everyone was very positive and encouraging. We made such a great couple. We got on so well.

A kind of madness overtook us, in which it seemed so much easier, in spite of the misgivings that neither of us had the heart to voice to the other, simply to go ahead rather than cause everyone the trouble of putting a stop to the proceedings.

Our plans went forward, all of them wholly unreal to me— ordering the invitations, making up the guest lists, choosing the food and the wine. I was playing the role of the Bride-to-Be, another interesting role that didn't seem to have any true bearing on my actual self. The Bride-to-Be Caroline was getting married, and then after we'd had our bit of fun with all that, we'd get back to whatever our true lives were slated to be. A half-hour before the service was to begin, I sprinted up the lawn of the church in shorts and a T-shirt, my dress slung over my shoulder. Got to get in makeup for the show—curtain in thirty minutes.

And so, with both of us smiling at each other and thinking to ourselves, *This is a serious mistake,* we vowed our lifelong devotion in a lovely little wedding on a perfect August day.

"Get closer to each other," complained Howie the photographer as we posed for the postceremony pictures. "You're supposed to be in love."

Three years later, a judge of the Circuit Court of the City of Richmond signed off on our divorce.

In the interim, we'd made a game go of it, but adulthood hadn't proved to be anything like what we'd been, all our lives, imagining it would. We expected, I suppose, fascinating careers, and exquisite, architecturally dynamic apartments, and dinner parties with intriguing friends—life like one of those wine commercials, with delighted laughter and the warm glow of candlelight and eager conversation carried on as you lounge casually on the arm of your shabby-chic sofa. Not jobs you feel half-ashamed to admit to and spaghetti for dinner every night in front of the TV in your non-descript suburban apartment complex and wondering if everything you could ever look forward to had already happened.

We spent most of our marriage ricocheting from crisis to crisis—of identity or career or goals or ambitions. Should we go to graduate school? What kind of graduate school? Should we be lawyers? Psychologists? Realtors? Teachers? Should we stay in our jobs? Change jobs? Move? Stay put? Stay married? Get a divorce? Should we change our sexual orientation? Our furniture? Our hairstyles? The cat box? Should we take up running? Unitarianism? Computer science? Should we write? Would we write? What would we write? There was no center that would hold, no true north to keep us from drifting in endless, disoriented circles, not a thing either of us could point to and say with confidence, *This is an absolute.*

We took grown-up jobs, office jobs, the kind of jobs we thought reasonable and responsible adults with education loans to pay off should take. We were too gifted in our capacity to imagine in vivid detail the worst potential consequences of risk to consider any other option. No ambling around Europe with a dollar in our pockets. No coffee-shop jobs and writing poetry in the mornings. I worked in insurance claims. He worked in commercial banking. We prided ourselves on how responsible we were. We wore responsibility like a hair shirt.

I had a nightmare once, when I was very young, at the culmination of which I stood smiling, said, "Yes sir," with agreeable resignation, and was promptly run over by a truck. That was my future ex-husband and me, putting on our business suits every morning, reporting to our respective offices, frozen smiles on our faces and despair icing our hearts, looking into a future that was nothing but another and another trip to the Safeway and *Santa Barbara* recorded on the VCR, and jobs that drove us nearly suicidal with boredom, and plodding unhappily around the mall every weekend asking, *Is this all there is?*

Our lives cried out for the geographical solution. Run away. Give up. Start again. But we stayed on the bus of our obligations, and another week passed, and another week passed in a kind of stunned torpor, and in this manner eventually three years passed, until at last we realized that we were no longer buoying each other up but rather drowning together. In the autumn following our third anniversary we got a nice, amicable divorce.

I ought to have felt at *least* a sense of failure at the dissolution of my marriage, but it all seemed so removed from me, just like the wedding we'd started with. It wasn't really my life, anyway. All I remember is relief that no more effort would be expected of me in this regard.

I was disentangling myself piece by piece, severing my obligations. I wanted less and less to be asked of me. You sometimes hear stories of people who fall into icy lakes and survive drowning because their metabolisms slow to the barest possible level of functioning. That's what I did with my life, a kind of icing down to the survivable minimum.

Part Three

29

Was it really that life was worse—that *I* was worse—than ever before, or was it just that now I had nothing left to distract me? For as long as I could remember, I'd relied upon school to provide the rhythm and the structure and the meaning to life. Your marks defined your value. School exercised your mind, distracting it from itself. The steady progression upward from elementary to middle to high school to college fostered the comforting notion that life was an evenly spaced series of ascensions.

Without school, even time itself had come unstrung, robbed of its structure. Wasn't it meant to run in 4/4 time, with a rest on the fourth note of summer? And wasn't autumn meant to be every year's beginning, a clean slate upon which to write your new self, swagged out in your back-to-school wardrobe still vaguely perfumed with the department store's essence? In school, you could continue to believe that no matter how badly last year had gone, this year might be an opportunity for everything to go differently, and on that belief had depended the optimism that it remained worth seeing what the future might hold.

Now in this disappointing adult life—a life I'd been scammed into looking forward to as the culmination, not the sorry purgatorial aftermath, of all those school years—there was no future, no past. Time just kept lurching along in a dreary, monotonous sameness of day and month and year. Like living in a whiteout.

Now, I spent my hours at work stunned, like someone beaten to the point of immobility, and rushed out the door at the end of the day only to spend the evening in solitude, listening to my mind race around in a random, shrieking, undistractable chaos.

I was driving myself crazy.

At twenty-five, I'd spent over half my life being—what? Depressed? Anxious? Muddled? Was there a name, even, for a chronic, restless uneasiness punctuated by suffocating intrusions of despair?

By now, I couldn't remember ever having felt any other way. I wasn't certain that I ever had felt any other way. It was almost impossible to imagine that there might *be* any other way to feel.

A creeping uneasiness, like kudzu, had completely overgrown my mind. "Free-range anxiety," I called it, and with neither apparent cause nor resolution it simply adapted itself to the circumstances at hand, worrying at every moment of my day like a penitent fingering a rosary.

I had become like some parlor game, a prodigy of dread; give me the topic and I'd find the worry in it. I worried about global warming, and about the short-tempered customer who'd cursed me that morning, about whether the roof would leak in the next rainstorm, and whether I'd worked out long enough to be entitled to eat dinner, and whether the cats were overdue at the vet's, and how long it had been since my car had its last oil change, and why call-in radio shows seemed so full of hate, and what the consequences might be for my body, the environment, and the future of humankind if instead of making dinner I just composed a salad in a nonrecyclable plastic container at the local grocery-store salad bar.

I had become obsessively preoccupied in particular with this disturbing interconnectivity of things, the way the most insignificant of decisions might have ramifications you could never know about when you made them. You stop for gas at the 7-Eleven and thereby miss getting hit by a car that runs the red light in the intersection you would have been crossing if you hadn't stopped. At the last minute you decide to go to the movie and step into the lobby just as the disgruntled ex-boyfriend of the popcorn girl opens fire with his semiautomatic.

I found it paralyzingly difficult to make even the simplest decisions. So much hung in the balance, so many complicated parameters needed to be taken into consideration, yet always there was too little information, no way to know what outcomes could result. Life was a terrifying, invisible web of consequences. What mayhem might I unknowingly wreak by saying yes when I could have said no, by going east instead of west?

Some girl, perky and fit in her aerobics gear, would stand beside me at the salad bar, scooping up tuna and pickled beets and shredded carrots without apparent thought and I'd want to scream, *HOW CAN YOU DO THAT?*

It was exhausting, enervating to struggle thus with every simple thing, every decision generating a hundred corollary decisions taking me farther and farther away from the original issue. My head wriggled and scurried frantically, like an ant mound in a panic. At home, in the eighty-year-old house whose irresponsible purchase was the last gesture of that ill-advised marriage, I spent hours pacing from window to window, maddeningly restless, paralyzingly indecisive.

I need to go, get away, go somewhere, I thought.

Where would I go? What would I do? I thought next. I never could think of the place, the action that suggested it might satisfy this nagging itchiness.

I should sort my laundry, I'd think. I'd contemplate the tangled, jumbled heap, imagine the effort required to distinguish light from bright from dark from white. Was this blue-and-white-striped shirt a dark or a bright or a white? When does khaki cross the threshold from light to dark? Where in the spectrum do I place a guacamole-green sweater? Each load must be large enough to justify the sacrifice of a few more gallons of the earth's too-little-valued water. Acknowledging that ultimately there was no such justification, that Americans were piggish in our squandering and polluting of the world's resources all in the ironic quest for some mythical, Edenic state of "mountain fresh" cleanliness. We washed our clothes too often. We had too many clothes. *I* had too many clothes. Why was I spending any money on clothes that just had to be cleaned, when every dollar spent was another dollar's worth of time I'd be condemned to labor in insurance?

And so it went. It was too much. It was beyond coping with.

Was this what it was like to go crazy, I wondered? Not a sudden splashing into the ocean of madness, but a creeping by degrees, a slow immersion?

I tried to cut my way out of this quagmire. With no husband to keep watch over my skin, it was easy to flick a line or two into the curve of bicep or thigh. What good did the cuts do me, however? At best, they earned me a few hours' respite; at worst, no more than a few minutes'.

There are self-mutilators who say with anguished resignation that they fully expect to end up dead within a few years; whatever you are trying to cut yourself free of, eventually you realize that with every cut you buy yourself just that much less time.

I can't go on, I thought.

But I did. I always did. Unable to imagine how I might do otherwise, I went on doing what I thought was expected of me. I went through the motions of life. I had one or two friends with whom I managed an occasional movie, and a desultory sort of boyfriend who virtually vanished six days out of the week, reappearing each Saturday so I could make him dinner. At work I played comic relief, making my alleged life the subject of a running patter for my co-workers. My crumbling house, its perpetually unattended renovation projects and dispirited urban environs, my absentee boyfriend and my on-the-spot ex-husband who still dropped by to do his laundry, the car that was always coughing up bizarre and costly mechanical ailments—all these were woven into a farcical narrative at the center of which a character bearing my name fumbled along in chronic ineptitude.

This brisk and bright public self was so damningly successful that for a period of time she was patently being groomed for a managerial position at work, buffed and primed to lead in a business that I loathed down to the last twist of my DNA. Worse yet, I actually tried to live up to this expectation, so as not to disappoint my groomers.

I wanted to give up. Ten times a day I wanted to give up. I craved giving up. I would read, almost longingly, stories of nervous breakdowns and suicides and wonder, *How did they muster the nerve to default on their obligations?* Where would you begin such an abdication?

One Sunday out of an indistinguishable series of Sundays parading before and behind me, I stood in the bathroom with blood dripping from my earlobe. A blank, emotionless face stared back at me from the mirror. She could have been no more than a vaguely familiar stranger, someone you pass on the street who makes you think ever so briefly, *Where have I seen that face before?*, but who, in a moment, you have forgotten. Her eyes were the gray-green of the ocean on a blustering winter day, and they studied me impassively.

How could she be so flat, so affectless?

Wake up! I demanded of her. I smeared blood across her cheek, her throat. My fingers left smudgy stains on her skin.

I will take this razor to that face, I will hack and slash down to the blood and bone and structure until I find something I can recognize. I will tear away this agreeable Caroline, this fucking responsible Caroline who is never anything but what she thinks is expected of her.

I stung the curve of my cheekbone with a hairline scratch, barely visible.

How much would it take to buy me giving up? How much to get off the bus? With my face in tatters, surely at last I couldn't be expected to go to work?

In my mind I had constructed a fantasy of place, the refuge for those with the courage to give up. I could hear the squeak of rubber soles on tile, the rattle of gurney wheels, the soothing patter of medicalspeak being traded over my head. Crisp white sheets and crisp white walls and nurses padding crisply down the hallway in their nurse's sneakers. I could lie there, clean, white, empty.

Only, I knew already what would happen, as inevitable as choosing the slowest-moving line at the grocery store. I'd be plugged in with some roommate—some girl in a religious mania, no doubt. She'd have that dazed, dreamy codeine look of the born-again overdose, and she'd babble on day and night about how Jesus told her the CIA had bugged her toaster oven, so that instead of lying there, suspended in pristine emptiness, I'd be perched co-operatively on the edge of my bed politely nodding. Then they'd haul me before a psychiatrist who would probe for the dark and desperate torments that had driven me to shred my face.

And I would have to confess, "I didn't like my job."

I put down the razor. The bus rolled on.

I could never get past the conviction that life had not entitled me to fall apart.

30

Under the influence of the seldom-seen boyfriend, who was a bicycle racer, I'd taken up competitive cycling. Well, to be entirely
accurate, I had taken only a brief stab at actual competition, hating
the nauseated pre-race jitters, hating the grim jockeying for position
at twenty-five miles an hour that could lead in an instant to a
sudden, disastrous conflation of wheels and limbs, and a broken
collarbone as the upshot. Nevertheless, I continued training, under
the self-perpetuated delusion of an imminent return to competition.

Cycling is like a time-share condo sales pitch; you're lured in
by the offer of some nice little freebie and before you know it
you've signed away the next twenty years of your life. I started
bicycling because it offered me the illusion of doing something
meaningful and productive with my life, while burning calories in

the bargain, and then I found that I couldn't stop. I was in fact afraid to stop, afraid that thirty miles or more a day was the only thing standing between me and the sudden gain of enormous amounts of weight, afraid that riding myself to exhaustion every night was the only thing keeping the baying hounds of dread from overrunning my life entirely. Instead, of course, exercise overran my life, one obsession traded for another traded for another. When I wasn't riding I was thinking about riding, I was preparing to ride or recovering from a ride or calculating and recalculating the number of carbohydrates and fat-free calories I'd consumed to be counterbalanced by a ride, I was standing in front of the mirror critically appraising the cut and delineation of quadriceps and gluteus, and finding myself wanting.

One evening then, in the dead of winter, I was racing along on my bicycle after dark, my way lit by the thin light of my headlamp, when a car turned suddenly in front of me. Headed downhill at the moment of impact, I hit my brakes but still slammed into the side of the car at maybe twenty miles an hour, just me and a few pounds of steel alloy and rubber. The impact spun me around, my head whipping like the tail end in a game of crack-the-whip to connect with the pavement with a dizzying SMACK! that split my helmet into a dozen pieces.

I lay there on the pavement in a strange bliss, utterly reduced to the stillness of Now. The cold air draped gently across my skin like a freshly laundered sheet. The taillights of the car that had hit me burned red like embers fifty feet away as the driver hesitated, then flickered and slunk off into the darkness.

Ah, hit and run, I thought, delighted with the playful whimsy of the phrase. Hit and run. Hitandrun.

I should get up. I really should. I should get up out of the street. Only it was so pleasant just to lie there, without worry or desire, without yesterday or tomorrow.

I have been waiting for years, I thought, *to be hit by this car.*

A couple walking their dog hurried up.

"We saw the whole thing," said the woman.

"I can't believe that car just drove away!" said the man.

"Hit and run," I said.

Their presence broke the bliss of the moment; considerations and preoccupations began creeping in like water rising in a slowly sinking boat.

The helpful couple helped me, limping, to the curb. My bicycle lay twisted and mangled under the orange glow of the street lamp.

My ankle ached, and I thought rapidly, with some eagerness, *If it's broken, I will not have to ride. If it's broken, maybe I will be ordered to rest. If it's broken, maybe I will be kept out of work.*

It wasn't broken. It wasn't even sprained. The emergency room doctor didn't even bother to wrap it, didn't even bother with the perfunctory prescription painkiller. "Tylenol as needed for discomfort," he scribbled almost illegibly on his orders pad, already walking out the door of the exam room. Out in the desolate hospital parking lot, I eased myself stiffly into the driver's seat of my car.

"Is there anyone I can call for you?" the policeman had asked me earlier after giving me a ride home, my broken bicycle stuffed in the trunk of the cruiser.

No, there really wasn't.

Three weeks later I stood in my kitchen, staring blankly at a can of soup in my hand. Its meaning completely eluded me. From instinct, I'd plucked it off the kitchen shelf—but what was it, and what did I mean to do with it?

At last with a mental *ping!* I understood, *Ah, this is soup!* and the meaning of soup came through to me, as though my understanding had just now arrived after a lengthy detour through a distant and difficult terrain.

This wasn't the first incident in which once-familiar objects were rendered incomprehensible. A few days before, I'd run a stop sign, getting halfway across the intersection before I understood what that red octagonal shape at the crossroads was meant to tell me. There were other moments, disconcerting and yet oddly fascinating, as though my thoughts had been transformed into some clanking Rube Goldberg device, the process between seeing and understanding laid bare before me.

The rage, however—that was only disconcerting. Never one with much use for anger, I'd found myself over these last few weeks apparently undertaking a precise cataloguing of anger's every nuance and particular, from frustration's brief flare to a blinding, seething, white-hot rage. With my first waking thought in the morning, anger roiled over me like an acid bath, and I'd imagine shooting myself in a welter of gore and viscera splattered across the muted gray of my comforter. In the morning commute I'd sit simmering in traffic, choked with loathing at poky drivers and ill-timed stoplights. At work I stabbed at my keyboard, spat out a good morning like a curse to every caller, and entertained the urge to grab up my letter opener and plunge it into my gut with a defiant shriek.

"You just don't seem like yourself lately," said my manager, in an unintended piece of irony. When had I ever seemed myself?

"Maybe you should see a doctor," she suggested. "Maybe when you hit your head in that accident you did some kind of damage."

Having digested a recounting of my symptoms, my doctor sent me for an MRI. I lay in the tube, lulled by the hypnotic, staccato racket of the machine. Afterward, I lingered in the radiologist's booth watching gray-scale images of my brain clicking on and off the screen.

"Well, I guess that proves I actually have one," I joked to the technician.

I couldn't take my eyes off the screen. When do you ever get to see your brain? It is the secret kept from you, the hand inside the puppet. Hemisphered and rippled, my brain looked just like . . . a brain. An organ, a lump of tissue, so textbook accurate it hardly seemed possible it could be *my* brain. I don't know quite what I'd expected. Psychedelic colors, or swirls of gray stabbed by pulses of light, like a thunderstorm seen from above?

Here was the place where all that is self resides, in its casing of flesh and bone. My fears and fancies, the dreaming and the dread, the hectoring and the hope. In what magnetically sliced cross-section might I see the tangled knot of my thoughts, like last year's Christmas lights boxed in the attic—the fretting and brooding and endlessly replicating worries? I stood there and waited for my precisely mapped and subdivided brain to reveal something, while frame after frame slipped silently across the screen.

―――――――

"Doesn't appear to be anything wrong," said my doctor, consulting the manila folder he carried. Not, at least, anything you could spot with a machine.

I slouched on the edge of his examining table, my legs dangling in space, the paper cover crinkling beneath me each time I shifted position.

"I'd like to try a short course of antidepressants," he said brightly, nonchalantly, tucking a pen into his lab coat pocket.

I was flabbergasted. Truly astonished by this wholly unanticipated tack in the conversation.

Depression? I thought.

I'd taken those depression indicator tests: *I am less happy than I used to be.* Well, sure, if by "used to be" the test meant when I was ten. I couldn't think of a time in the last decade, in the last fifteen years, when I could say I'd been happy. It's not that I had been always *un*happy, just that chronic, insidious anxiousness robbed the color from things and left me a world dressed in muted, muddy tones. Simple, unqualified pleasure eluded me. But could I call that depression? No, my life was more like a flat Coke—flavor minus the fizz.

My doctor was offering me a definition, a diagnosis, something I could hang my hat on and name, after all these long years I'd spent coveting some stamp of authentication, and all I could think was that I didn't qualify to be depressed.

Surely he's going to figure this out in a minute, I thought. What was the point in stepping up to the plate just to swing at a bad pitch?

I'd say, "Oh sure, hit me with them antidepressants, doc," and then he'd pause, maybe do a double-take, then study me sorrowfully, as though I were a once-promising honors student found helping myself to the marching band's candy sales fund.

"Antidepressants?" he'd say. "Oh no no no, young lady, not for the likes of you. And aren't you a little old for these self-important histrionics? Now run along home, and stop taking up Doctor's time when people who really need me are waiting."

I changed the subject, and he let it slide, which only confirmed my suspicion that he hadn't really meant it in the first place. It was one thing to fret and pace and think about killing yourself over your laundry, and it was another thing to be so self-indulgent as to believe that your whiny, narcissistic, middle-class preoccupations amounted to anything of substance.

31

This is the kind of story that wouldn't be complete without the requisite round of therapy, so let me just go right ahead and cut to the chase: I went into therapy. Actually, to be precise, I went in and out of therapy over the next half-dozen years or so, like someone stuck in a revolving door.

My ex-husband convinced me to go the first time. He said I should go, and I said don't be ridiculous, and he said it would do me a world of good, and I said how could I go into therapy when there wasn't anything legitimately wrong with me, and he said how could I say there wasn't anything wrong with me when I cut up my skin to make myself feel better, and I said yes but maybe I only cut myself because I thought it made me seem more like someone who could say there was something legitimately wrong with herself and you couldn't discount my flair for melodrama just overdoing things a bit.

Anyway, he won, and I went, maybe all of four times, before claiming to this first counselor that I was going on vacation and then never calling back again.

Another year or so went by, and I dragged myself in to the next therapist in the series. With each new counselor, M.S.W. or M.Ed. or L.C.S.W. or Ph.D., I'd find myself waiting for the denunciation as one cringing in anticipation of a painful blow.

"Don't waste my time," I kept expecting them to say. "I'm here for people with *real* problems."

Perhaps you'll find it odd that never, in any of these successive rounds in the psychotherapeutic ring, did I go with the express intent of addressing the cutting. Instead, I went because—I don't know exactly why I went. I went because there's something fatally seductive about being granted license to talk about yourself virtually nonstop for an hour. I went because I wanted to see if I could learn to inhabit my own life, and not just watch it from the wings like a stage manager. I went because I kept holding out the hope that one of these high priests of sanguinity could consult the Talmudic authority of the *Diagnostic and Statistical Manual of Mental Disorders* and pronounce my case the way an auto mechanic avers "bad shocks" or "loose struts," and, armed with a pinpointed diagnosis, fix me up quick. I was looking for the cheap miracle, something as absolute as the instantaneous division between Before and After that could be wrought with a cut—but permanent. Some door I could step through, some new life I could put on like a new suit of clothes, leaving my former self forever and irrevocably behind.

I went through five therapists in as many years. I'd improve marginally, leave therapy, and backslide even further. Then eventually I'd start over again, until I got to feeling as if I should just type up a résumé of my dysfunctions and hand it over wordlessly to each new counselor, so we could skip the preliminaries and get down to business.

———

During the thick of this therapeutic back-and-forthing, I met the man with whom I would eventually take an improbably optimistic second shot at marriage. When we met—I standing on my front porch, he on the sidewalk at the far end of a sofa he was helping carry for his friend, my newly-acquired-via-the-want-ads roommate—what struck me almost immediately about him was his determined good cheer. He looked on life, I soon found, as great fun, a highly amusing adventure in which things were bound to turn out all right in the end, and in the meantime you could look forward to all sorts of unanticipated delights and pleasurable surprises. Whereas I'd been accustomed to regarding life as a rigged examination I was imminently likely to fail.

He was a believer in daydreams and long shots. He'd go with your idea, however farfetched. Things could be done. Anything might be accomplished. "Don't let life get in the way" was his policy.

He was, in short, an extremely unlikely match for me, but from the start I found something infectious about his enthusiasm, when all my life I'd known mostly people inclined to take the grim view of things. He made it all look so easy. If his influence didn't actually make me enthusiastic, it did at least make me consider enthusiasm possible.

Under the spell of his optimism, I at last quit my hateful job, after seven years, five months, and four days. Wailing predictions of certain disaster, financial ruin, and lifelong unemployability all the way, nevertheless I quit. I went back to graduate school. I reimmersed myself in language and literature as one who has been wandering the desert plunges bodily into the welcome, cooling waters of an oasis. I ought to have been deliriously happy. I wasn't.

Instead, I cycled from elation to despair at a dizzying rate that left me stunned and exhausted—sometimes, in the course of one three-hour seminar, I rocketed back and forth between these extremes a half-dozen times or more. My public self, meanwhile, somehow managed to continue attending and contributing intelligently to the classroom discussion. The two almost entirely unrelated personae uneasily cohabited within my flesh.

I had dreamed for years of a life comprising only long hours of solitude and a thick stack of books, but now, when at home, I found my anxieties racing out to fill the enormous silence, churning it into a turbulent sea of worry. I was paralyzed by anxiety, too restless to stay still, too indecisive to move.

When you date someone, and she haltingly confesses that she's in therapy, this patina of angst endows her with a certain poetic glamour. But when you marry her, and get to live day and night with the reasons *why* she is in therapy, angst loses a good measure of its appeal.

"You don't cut anymore, though, do you?" he'd asked once early in our relationship, the question one that we would revisit again and again in the coming years.

A quandary: the truthful answer, or the answer that would make him happy? I didn't want to repeat all my past mistakes. I didn't want to continue the self-editing and the half-truths and the seamless evasions. But to say no, I no longer cut, though it would make him happy, would not be entirely the truth. I still cut, sometimes. On the other hand, to admit that I was not entirely an ex-self-mutilator, though the truth, would not make him happy.

I chose the frank equivocation, the honest half-truth, the candidly evasive answer:

"You know, the cutting doesn't have anything to do with you. It's not about you. It's not because of you. It's an old, old history."

"But you won't do it anymore," he said, not so much a question as the salesman's assumed close.

Here in the course of only a minute's dialogue was precisely the reason I had always avoided honesty, why honesty was not a good idea: the impossible promise, the promise you make for the promisee's peace of mind and not your own.

He was a project guy, a tackle-a-problem-and-fix-it guy, and he felt he ought to be able to fix me, too.

"I know you say it doesn't have anything to do with me," he

said, "but if you cut now I can't help feeling like somehow I'm responsible."

"Why does it have to be about *your* feelings?" I wanted to say resentfully. Why did I have to give up what I needed in order to make him happy?

"It's so destructive," he said.

"But it isn't," I insisted. "It's not about hurting or punishing myself. It's not like I'm drinking or doing drugs—that's destructive."

"It is destructive. It hurts me."

"But it doesn't have anything do to with you!" I said, exasperated.

"Of course it does! It might not be my fault, but I can't just sit there and say it's no big deal to me if you're cutting yourself up with razor blades."

At the time, his position annoyed me. It struck me as unreasonable and overly alarmist. Too stuck on his perspective and insufficiently sympathetic to mine. After all, I'd been cutting for the better part of two decades, and no one else among the few who knew about it had ever made a fuss. Even my counselors, when I sprang it on them, had merely nodded gravely, not even a trace of a wince or a twitch of an eyebrow to suggest undue concern.

I was surprised, taken aback, then, by the expectation implicit in his stubborn refusal just to let the matter slide—the expectation that love obligated me to consider *his* feelings on the issue. I'd always believed that a relationship was dedicated, above all else, to the equable preservation of an undisturbed peace, and that all parties to the relationship tacitly conspired toward this end. You didn't volunteer information no one else wanted, and they didn't ask questions they didn't want to hear the answers to. Now here was this man blundering recklessly across the rules of engagement, and how was I to respond?

———

One of those long, empty afternoons, when I ought to have been reading my way through a few hundred pages of *Clarissa* for my next day's seminar in the eighteenth-century novel, I sat curled up instead in the threadbare easy chair in my study. The chair was one my parents had bought before I was born, comfortably familiar in its frayed upholstery sprouting tufts of some silky, pre-kapok stuffing. The three o'clock light of a winter afternoon—the light of sinking depression—dropped listlessly through my window, and I could feel my spirits sagging with the declining angle of the sun.

At that moment, an understanding that had been coming together slowly in my mind for years suddenly coalesced: that the exhausted light of late afternoon *always* depressed me. It ought to have been the most obvious fact in the world, but I had never understood it clearly until this moment.

With this realization, one edge, one absolutely reliable fact was laid against the otherwise apparently featureless miasma of my unhappiness.

I suppose I'd always imagined that someday, somehow, I would rid myself completely of this unhappiness like one shrugging off a sweater—that some change in the geography of my life, or the achievement of some magical inner circle of therapeutic accomplishment, would put it fully and irrevocably behind me. Now, however, I could see that my revenant despairs had their own pattern, that as surely as they receded, so they would return, but that just as they would inevitably return, so they would once again recede. The respite might not come for days, maybe even weeks. It might last only a moment, or it might settle in for days on end, so that it became difficult to remember the precise features of unhappiness.

Somehow, however, just knowing that I could fully expect unhappiness to return—if not predictably, then nevertheless reliably—was strangely liberating. The point was that even chaos had a structure, a beginning and eventually an end. It was possible to live through it. I'd been doing as much for twenty years.

Somehow, too, in recognizing that something so arbitrary as the tenor of winter light had the power to disrupt my entire emotional circuitry, I found an odd relief. Maybe unhappiness wasn't something you had to qualify for through a suitable measure of suffering. Maybe unhappiness *was* my suffering.

I remembered the afternoon of my MRI, the way I'd seen my brain that day for what it is—an organ. A lump of tissue and cells and nerves, no less than heart or lungs or kidney, generating perception as much as the heart pumps blood or the lungs extract oxygen. How we know and feel and understand the world is made possible merely by the pulse of electrochemical activity. If a heart could fail in its pumping, a lung in its breathing, then why not a brain in its thinking, rendering the world forever askew, like a television with bad reception? And couldn't a brain fail as arbitrarily as any of these other parts, without regard to how fortunate your life might have been, without regard to the blessing and cosseting that, everyone was so eager to remind you, disentitled you from unhappiness?

32

I can say that there's something perversely comforting in knowing that even unhappiness has its own reliability. Nevertheless, looking forward only to another and another and another bout of misery was not, in the long view, the most cheering of prospects. Knowing that my tortuous anxieties might be nothing more than the product of the odd twitch and spasm of my brain did not a whit to modify their control of my life.

Then one day the latest of my counselors suggested, as I was itemizing for her yet another example of the agonizingly tortured process of my thoughts, "I'm not suggesting you could take a pill and all this would go away, but have you ever thought about antidepressants?"

I'd been down this road before.

"I'm not depressed!" I protested. "Not 'Ten Warning Signs of Depression' depressed."

Well, she didn't think I was depressed, exactly, either. But she'd been reading the latest research on the newest class of antidepressants—the selective serotonin reuptake inhibitors, or SSRIs.

"There's some promising evidence that they can help with anxiety, obsessive thoughts, that kind of thing."

This time, I was ready to consider the pharmacological tune-up. I was ready to consider almost anything that might stem the relentless tide of my thoughts. My thoughts flogged me like an overseer among the galley slaves, compelling me onward in a continuous, panicked flight to nowhere. So I went to talk to my counselor's consulting psychiatrist.

He was old enough to be my father, nearing retirement, his manner suggesting that he'd seen quite enough and then some in his long psychiatric career. Instead of making him world-weary and cynical, however, his experience seemed to have taught him to appreciate the high hilarity and essential absurdity of the human condition. He radiated a satisfied amusement with the irrationality of things. You could tell him you cut yourself with razor blades, and you would not disturb his equanimity. He'd just nod with great interest, occasionally drawing you forth with a succinct and thought-provoking question.

For an hour I downloaded my history, cramming it all together in an unbroken stream so that even to me it did start to sound collectively disturbed. At the end of this hour during which he had drawn me forth with succinct and thought-provoking questions, he handed me a sheaf of papers, checklists on anxiety and depression and obsessive-compulsive disorders—dysfunctional potluck. I felt oddly excited, as if I'd won the mental illness lottery; the man was an M.D., a psychiatrist with years of experience under his belt. He couldn't be wrong, he could spot a wacko at fifty paces, and he'd conferred on me the irrefutable stamp of the legitimately unbalanced.

I left his office with my little stack of papers clutched close to my chest, and on top of them all a featherweight box of samples: Paxil. Like peace. Like peaceful. I had joined the nation of the selective serotonin reuptake inhibited.

I began with a tiny dose, breaking the crumb-sized pill into quarters. I felt as though I were holding my breath, not knowing what I was waiting for or what to expect or how I would know if it worked, or when it worked, or indeed what "working" would mean.

I was still waiting, when it dawned on me, after a week or so, that the endless harangue, like a screaming argument, that had carried on in my head for years had died away. I could still hear it, but it was as though the parties to the disagreement had moved off down the hall, leaving me behind to think, *My, that certainly is a contentious debate and I'm glad it's none of my concern.* I felt as if a huge space had been cleared in my life, as if I'd been sharing a room for years with an unruly crowd of surly roommates who played their stereos too loud, and they'd all suddenly moved out.

In the absence of all that noise and confusion, I was overwhelmed by a sudden explosion of energy; there were a million wonderful, engaging things I wanted to see and do and discover, and I wanted to try all of them right now.

I couldn't pinpoint any specific thing about my life that had changed, but I felt as though I had emigrated to some other world. For the first time I understood how you could sit down at a meal and not be so busy fretting about the food and eating it and not eating it that you missed most of the conversation. I could pick up a quart of milk without feeling as though the entire fate of humankind hung in the balance between choosing the store brand or the national brand. I could make a decision, and it seemed neither complicated nor difficult to do so; you weighed certain obvious factors, and then you decided.

Well, what did all this mean for me? What did it say about the anxiety and unhappiness that had clouded and wasted the preceding two decades of my life? Had I been denied the true potential of over half my life for the sake of a short measure of serotonin? Was it truly possible, by means of a mere dose of chemistry, to unzip the suit of your old life and step into something entirely new?

This happiness, this ease of mind, was too easy. I didn't trust it. It came too cheap. More confusing yet was what I never would have expected—I felt the absence of the familiar hue and cry of my mind, and if I can't say that I missed it precisely, at any rate I sensed a loss of the depth and texture it had lent to my life.

Not that any of these misgivings, mind you, would have led me to give Paxil up, but in the end I forsook it anyway; doing that, I said, was like being rescued after weeks at sea in an open lifeboat, and then, after a wonderful meal and a shower and a night spent in a luxuriously comfortable bed, being informed the next morning that you would be returned to the lifeboat and set adrift once more.

I was giving up Paxil with the intention of becoming pregnant; I didn't want to simmer my theoretical baby in a synthetic chemical stew. The ironic thing is that I might never have mustered the absurd optimism to believe that having a baby was a good idea if I hadn't been soaking myself all these weeks in the benign bath of my own serotonin. Why was I thinking of having a baby? Who could rationally contemplate bringing a child into this terrible, care-worn world? Was I in any manner qualified for such a grave responsibility, I who could spend a whole day just mustering the conviction to get to the grocery store?

In the heart of my Paxilated tranquillity, all these objections struck me as trifling, but as I weaned myself week by week, their significance mushroomed. By the time (still within hailing distance of the last molecular gasp of my Paxil) the two purple lines on the home test kit confirmed my pregnancy, I was possessed by the conviction that I'd made a terrible, terrible mistake. What madness had gripped me, obscuring the obvious fact that I didn't even particularly *like* babies? I'd always been the first to execute a discreet exit, stage left, when someone at the office appeared, mid–maternity leave, with the tiny bundle in tow. I found the oozy-squoozy, pastel-pink cultural sentimentality surrounding pregnancy toxically repulsive.

I couldn't imagine myself like every other newly minted mother I'd seen, with my baby slung easily on an outthrust hip. I couldn't imagine myself pushing some as-yet-unrealized somebody on a swing or snapping photos of birthdays or saying mom things like "Don't track those muddy shoes all over my kitchen." Mothers were other people, grown-ups, women who could keep track of shots and shoes and play dates. I went through my entire pregnancy feeling I was trying to pull off a sham, pretending to the part of the ethereal madonna when I was wholly unqualified for the job.

And yet. When my son was born, into the waiting shelter of my arms, it was though the shape and structure of me had been made precisely to the purpose of fitting him. I was shocked by the fierce and immediate entanglement of this bond, that my son should become to me like a chamber of my heart.

———————

I brought him into this world, made him up from scratch and delivered him into this troubled and troubling world, so that someday, like all of the rest of us, he will suffer loss and grief and doubt. It is my responsibility, therefore, to believe that something else is possible as well. I have to believe that life will also offer him its gestures of grace.

Here's the part where I'm supposed to have the big epiphany: some climactic confrontation, a couple of weepy scenes, and then the tidy wrap-up, the denouement. Maybe I throw in a few twelve-step-meeting interludes where I tell you about Pam (not her real name) who is a striking blonde, an executive at a Fortune 500 company, who confesses to the group that on weekends she inscribes her Fortune 500 flesh with a box-cutter. Then I tell you how I'm in recovery, one day at a time.

I don't have a tidy narrative conclusion to offer. When I finally stopped cutting, there was no specific day I could mark for this turn, no moment of epiphany when everything became suddenly clear to me and I forsook the razor forever. Instead, the end came as a series of unconnected moments assembling themselves into a whole that is evident only in retrospect.

I started cutting because at a particular point in my life I ran afoul of a certain unique set of circumstances for which neither experience nor my own emotional constitution had equipped me. I can't say what precise conjunction of factors led me to choose self-mutilation as my recourse, nor can I say how my life might have been different if any one of these factors had been otherwise. All I can say is that my skin itself seemed to cry out for an absolution in blood.

I kept cutting, because it worked. When I cut, I felt better for a while. When I cut, my life no longer overwhelmed me. I felt too keenly the threat of chaos, of how things can get away from you in a thousand ways. Bodies expand, grades plummet, pets die, paint peels, ice caps melt, genocide erupts. Entropy keeps eating at the ramparts, and I cut to try to shore them up. I cut to lay down a line between before and after, between self and other, chaos and clarity. I cut as an affirmation of hope, saying, *I have drawn the line and I am still on this side of it.*

There's no explaining that by reason or logic, any more than you can measure grief with a mathematical equation or formulate memory in a test tube. Sometimes the mind just has its own ideas.

When I stopped cutting, it was only because I could afford to, because my need for it had apparently run its natural course, like the fever the body mounts to fight off an infection, that subsides when the danger is past. There are self-mutilators whose stories are much harder than mine; their wounds are much deeper, and their bodies look like the scarred-over field of a battle. Sometimes, after years of fighting, they end up losing the war. But if you make it to your thirties, suggests the assembled evidence on self-mutilation, then chances are good you'll have fought all the way through to some kind of truce, some resolution. You have the benefit of the simple luxury of time and perspective.

I could look back over the evidence of more than twenty years, marked in dozens of scars—some dark, some pale, some ribbed by the patch job of tissue that reconnected the severed fabric of my flesh, some almost too faint to announce themselves except as the most infinitesimal of breaks in the crosshatched pattern of my skin.

How many cuts could I count? How many could I place in time and context? I had to admit that I couldn't remember the occasion of almost any of them, their catalysts, whether epic or mundane, completely obscured by time. So many moments of supposedly unendurable pain, now utterly forgotten. You start to think, *Maybe I don't need this anymore.* Maybe I never did.

I stopped cutting because I always could have stopped cutting; that's the plain and inelegant truth. No matter how compelling the urge, the act itself was always a choice. I had no power over the flood tide of emotions that drove me to that brink, but I had the power to decide whether or not to step over. Eventually I decided not to.

Stopping, however, was not at all the same thing as ending the desire. Even now, I still sometimes ache with a fierce, organic need for cutting's seductive, minimalist simplicity. I expect that I will always be the kind of person who is too much aware of the boundlessness of chaos; it's like having an unfortunate sixth sense, alive to the teeming, invisible undercurrents of anarchy streaming past us at every moment. I don't say it makes me stronger, or more interesting, or gives me character; it's just a part of my fabric of self. Most days it makes me yearn at least once, and on the bad days almost constantly, for a leave of absence from my own life any way I can get it. But you get older, and you see that you have choices, and you see that you're only going to have this one life, and it's up to you whether you want to seize hold of it or leave it forever waiting in unclaimed baggage. If I could have understood this point earlier, maybe it would have saved me a lot of grief. Maybe, on the other hand, you have to make your journey, and bear its scars.

When I was planning for the birth of my son, I got one piece of advice about labor that stood me in greatest stead: A woman told me that the key is to focus on the contraction you're in, and not to think about the ones yet to come. That's what I'm trying to do with my life, to confront what faces me now, and recognize that I cannot know what else might come until it gets here. I try to understand that all we ever have at our disposal is the present, and in the present I can choose either to cut or not to cut.

Choosing not to cut has meant that instead I have had to sit there with the awful agony of unhappiness when it comes—with loneliness, loss, anger, regret, disappointment—and gut it through. The first few times, when I had a fight with my husband, when my cat died, when free-range anxiety swallowed me up whole, it was like having unanesthetized surgery. I had to keep screaming to myself above the shrieking of my distress, *THIS WILL NOT KILL YOU!*

Each time, I expected the looming offstage dread I'd been running from all my life to reveal itself at last, and bring the world down in pieces. To my surprise, instead, the terrible feelings would eventually, at last, come to an end, and I would find myself still intact. Maybe shaken and bruised a little, but still in one piece. I'd glance around almost amazed at life resuming its stride, as though I were crawling out of the storm cellar after a tornado to discover quite unanticipatedly that the house is still standing.

In that complex interplay of experience and physiology, I like to think that every time I gut it through and survive, I'm reshaping the structure and the chemistry of my thoughts, wearing new paths less tortured and convoluted than the old ones. Every new crisis successfully negotiated and survived inches me that much farther from the event horizon of despair.

I have drawn the line, and I am still on this side of it.

I would like to thank Sharon Brooks for generously granting me the time to write; Susan Shreve for many years of encouragement; my agent, Jennie Dunham, for her vision and invaluable advice; my editor, Reagan Arthur, for her patience and editorial guidance; Leslie Shiel; Wendi Kaufman; Joe and Lee Sites; my parents and extended family for all their support; and most of all my husband, for everything.